40 days

Thinking through Lent

Peter Dainty

kevin mayhew

First published in 2004 by

KEVIN MAYHEW LTD
Buxhall, Stowmarket, Suffolk, IP14 3BW
E-mail: info@kevinmayhewltd.com

9 8 7 6 5 4 3 2 1 0

ISBN 1 84417 317 8
Catalogue No. 1500736

Cover design by Angela Selfe
Edited and typeset by Katherine Laidler

Printed and bound in Great Britain

Contents

To Tom, Sam, Elly, Matthew and Hannah,
my lovable, lively grandchildren

Introduction

Lent is the season for spiritual spring cleaning – for turning out what is no longer useful, cleaning up or replacing what has become dirty and drab, and generally putting our spiritual house in order. It is a time to unload guilt and receive forgiveness, to ditch those moral bad habits which spoil our relationship with God and with others, to freshen up our religious habits if they have become stale and mechanical, and to renew our dedication to the service of God.

So Lent is a time for repentance. The Greek word for repent literally means to rethink, to think again, to change one's mind. Therefore, Lent is a time for some serious thinking. If our beliefs have got stuck in traditional terms that we take for granted but don't fully understand, it helps to think them through again. If our attitudes have been fashioned by 'what everybody else thinks', we should think them out for ourselves and not be content to live at second hand and second rate.

The aim of this book is to help the individual reader to meditate on the scriptures and perhaps see them with a fresh eye, so that their meaning and relevance become clearer. The passages to be considered are those selected from the Revised Common Lectionary for the principal services on Ash Wednesday and the five Sundays of Lent, plus the gospel for Palm Sunday. The selection covers the liturgical years A, B and C. These readings have been arranged for 40 days of study during Lent and cover a wide range of topics. Because there are 66 passages in all, two or three are often grouped together on one day under one heading because they share a common theme. The contents list and the biblical reference index will help readers to find their way around.

The arrangement for each day begins with a summary of the relevant Bible passage or passages. It is important to note that this is not a full translation and should be regarded only as an introduction to the study and not as a substitute for reading the complete passage in the Bible. The study which follows the summary offers a line of thought which is aimed at stimulating the reader's own thinking on the passage concerned and is certainly not meant to be the final word on the matter. The important thing is that by meditating on the different passages each day for 40 days, the reader will be able to think again about many aspects of the Christian faith and benefit spiritually from their meditations.

PETER DAINTY

Day 1: Ash Wednesday
A plague of locusts

Joel 2:1, 2, 12-17

The prophet Joel warns the people of an imminent disaster, which he compares to a plague of locusts but it could be any kind of destructive attack. He says this will be the dark Day of the Lord, and calls on all the people, young and old alike, to come together in penitence and turn to God for mercy. If they do, God may bless them with an abundant harvest.

The prophet's message reminds us that we are always living on the edge, though we in the developed countries don't always realise it. People who are all too familiar with plagues of locusts are more likely than we are to understand that disaster lurks round every corner and can strike at any moment. We live on a planet that provides us with all that we need for our survival, but we are also surrounded by powerful forces that aren't entirely under our control. And they can destroy our carefully nurtured wealth and wellbeing overnight.

The Israelites knew about plagues of locusts because their ancestors had seen them in Egypt in the time of slavery. But Joel is saying that it isn't only Egyptians who can suffer from them; Israelites can as well. Nor should we think we are immune from disasters in our modern affluent societies. They can be both natural and man-made. Having thought that with the end of the Cold War we had escaped the nuclear threat, we now find ourselves facing the mounting horror of terrorist threats, which, even if we never face one directly, eat away at our peace of mind.

Where have we gone wrong? That question is the beginning of penitence. To repent means to think again, not just as individuals but as communities. This is the social aspect of Lent, because Lent isn't just about individual penitence and self-examination. It's about communal penitence and self-examination. Are we running the world fairly? Are we sharing its wealth evenly? Are we seeking reconciliation or confrontation? Are we contributing to instability and uncertainty in the natural order by our careless use of the earth's resources? Are we witnessing a moral decline in our society which could become irreversible if we ignore it too long? Do we have to wait until there is another disaster before we do anything about these things? Perhaps we've witnessed enough disasters already but are still reluctant to act decisively and effectively.

Joel reminds us that our response to communal disasters has to be a communal one. He calls on all the community to gather together and turn to God for help. Everyone must show an earnest desire for radical change, not just by wearing torn clothes but by feeling the real pain of broken hearts. Our world community very often feels like a loose bundle of conflicting factions, none of which is happy to live alongside the others, and none of which is sorry – except for themselves. But God is merciful and may yet respond to our heartfelt cries and our genuine willingness to seek a way forward for the common good, by restoring the years that the locust has eaten.

Joel describes the Day of the Lord as a day of clouds and thick darkness. A swarm of locusts is very much like a thundercloud – dark and threatening. But God's prophets are like clouds as well, and we don't always welcome what they have to say because they uncover our failings and insecurities. We would rather concentrate on short-term negative solutions to our problems by targeting our enemies and destroying them before they can destroy us. However, this doesn't solve the underlying problems which created our enemies in the first place. It just creates more. The prophet Joel's solution requires penitence because then we start to take some responsibility for the world's problems instead of just blaming them on someone else.

Day 2: Thursday
True fasting

Isaiah 58:1-12

With a trumpet voice the prophet tries to awaken the people to their sins. They use prayer and fasting as a ritual by which they claim to be seeking God, but really they only seek God's blessing, not his will. Their fasting has become a farce because it only cloaks their disregard for social evils. The fast which God wants is one that inspires them to set free the oppressed, feed the hungry and provide for the homeless poor and the naked among them. Then the light will dawn upon them as they begin to build a just community.

The prophet is strongly critical of the people's limited understanding of fasting. They think of it as a kind of magical ritual which will convince God that they are truly penitent and persuade him to give them what they want. The popular modern understanding of fasting is equally limited. It is one of the ways in which we are happy to trivialise Lent, because it excuses us from thinking about more serious things. We give up sweets, we give up smoking, we give up TV (perhaps), but for what purpose? For the sake of our health? For the sake of feeling good inside? But what about the health of our society? What about the wellbeing of our community? If fasting makes me realise that I normally eat too much and need to cut down permanently; that smoking damages my health and the health of others; or that I watch too much TV and could devote my time to more creative activities, it will have done some good. But if it only makes me irritable and bad-tempered and not a more kindly and generous person, it is a useless ritual. And if it only eases my conscience and enables me to carry on living the same old thoughtless and self-centred life, it is worse than useless.

At the very least, fasting should help me to try and identify with those who have to struggle every day for every crumb they eat, and to turn that sense of identity into practical action on their behalf. Otherwise it isn't just a triviality – it's a mockery!

Real fasting is 'to live simply, so that others may simply live' – well-known words, and how easy they are to say. But how hard they are to put into practice, especially if we try to live like that all the time and not just in Lent.

Matthew 6:1-6, 16-21

Jesus condemns the ostentatious almsgiving, prayer and fasting of those who wish to be regarded as especially holy, and he teaches that personal piety should be practised in private, witnessed only by the Father.

The prophet gave us the basic meaning of genuine fasting, but Jesus is more lenient with us and doesn't dismiss the ritual of fasting out of hand. First, he puts it alongside almsgiving and prayer as an important aspect of religious life. Secondly, he says *'When* you fast', not *'If* you fast', assuming that we will fast, just as we will give alms and pray. (It's true that he didn't expect his disciples to fast while he was with them in the flesh, but when he was taken from them they would – Mark 2:19, 20). Thirdly, Jesus himself fasted in the wilderness, and that, of course, became the basis for the tradition of fasting during Lent in later times.

But it is easy to turn fasting into a mechanical formality with no moral or spiritual content, instead of an expression of genuine sorrow for our failures and weaknesses and a commitment to the demanding implications of our Christian faith. If fasting is to have any real value, it must lead us to make changes in our priorities and lifestyle and turn our attention away from ourselves towards God and towards others. But do it cheerfully – slick your hair and wash your face. There's no point in spreading gloom by looking miserable.

So let us listen to what the Lord says about fasting in Matthew 6, but let the words of the Lord in Isaiah 58 (and it's the same Lord who is speaking) reveal to us an even deeper truth.

Day 3: Friday
A bruised and broken heart

Psalm 51:1-17

David prays for forgiveness in anguished recognition that his sins have sprung from his own corrupt and tainted nature. He has nothing to bring but a guilty, broken heart as he gives himself up to the mercy of God.

This moving prayer is traditionally ascribed to David after his sin of adultery with Bathsheba, followed by the murder of her husband, Uriah. The whole dreadful story is told in 2 Samuel 11:1–12:25, including David's condemnation by the prophet Nathan and the subsequent death of Bathsheba's child. I hope Psalm 51 *was* David's penitential prayer because there is very little sign of his penitence in the story itself.

However, Psalm 51 provides fitting words for all who have been burdened by their guilt and turned to God for forgiveness. Even if our sins are not the same as David's, there are times when we know in our hearts that we have a corrupt and tainted nature and sometimes feel the awful pain of our own moral sickness. We also realise at such times that only God can help us and we cry out to him instinctively for forgiveness. The amazing thing is that God does forgive.

I can't improve on the words of the Psalm, but as it was originally Hebrew poetry, I've tried to give it a poetic feel in English, by the use of rhyme and rhythm.

O God, have mercy upon me,
for your love is deep, and kind, and strong.
O God, have mercy upon me,
and wipe out all my wrong;
please wipe out all my wrong.

My sin is ever before me,
like a painful cancer in my soul.
God, you are the one I've offended,
but you can make me whole;
only you can make me whole.

Yet you are right to condemn me;
your sword of guilt has pierced me through.
Lord, purge my degenerate nature,
and wash me white as snow;
as white as drifting snow.

Renew my spirit within me,
and give new life to my broken heart.
It is all I have to present you –
my trembling eager part;
my bruised and broken heart.

O God, have mercy upon me;
let me sing with joy and shout your praise.
O God, have mercy upon me,
and keep me in your ways;
stay with me all my days.

Day 4: Saturday
Forgiveness

John 8:1-11

Some scribes and Pharisees tried to test Jesus by bringing to him a woman who had committed adultery and asking him if he thought she should be stoned to death as the Law required. Jesus took charge of the situation by bending down and calmly writing in the dust with his finger. When they persisted with their question, he stood up and said to them, 'Let the one who throws the first stone be the one among you who is without sin.' Then he bent down again and continued writing in the dust with his finger. One by one, starting with the eldest, the scribes and Pharisees moved away until only Jesus was left, with the woman standing in front of him. He looked up and said to her, 'Woman, where have they gone? Doesn't anyone condemn you?' She said, 'No one, Lord.' Jesus said, 'Neither do I condemn you. Go, and sin no more.'

To get the full impact of this wonderful story you need to read the complete version in your Bible, and not just my summary, because almost every word is full of significance and descriptive power.

Immediately before this incident, Jesus was at the Mount of Olives, where he had probably spent all night in prayer (verse 1). Thus he was spiritually prepared for anything which he might have to face that day.

Then, early in the morning, he went to the Temple and began teaching the people (verse 2). The Temple was always important to Jesus, even from boyhood. It was then that he had sat among the teachers and amazed them with his understanding; now he was himself the Teacher and was still amazing those who listened to him. That is why the religious authorities were keen to trap him by asking him awkward questions. They were afraid of his popular appeal and his radical teaching, which seemed to threaten their establishment authority. So this woman caught in the act of adultery gave them a good opportunity for dispute. Did Jesus uphold the Law of Moses or not? It was a searching question.

But Jesus knew what they were about, and he also knew that the woman was of no real concern to them; she was simply a pawn in their game. In fact she was a vulnerable object in a world ruled by men. In committing adultery, *she* was the sinner, not the man. So Jesus paused and doodled on the ground to give himself a chance to think. His enemies were only thinking that they'd surely caught him this time, and they were impatient for his answer. But he didn't give them an answer. He simply replied with a searching suggestion: 'Let the one who throws the first stone be the one among you who is without sin.' Then he wrote in the sand again while they thought about it. Their question to him had appealed to his mind; it was an intellectual question. But Jesus appealed to their hearts: their consciences and their humanity. And one of the surprising things about the story is that the scribes and Pharisees showed that they had hearts by withdrawing one by one. And the eldest went first because he must have had more moral self-awareness than the rest, having had more experience of the dark side of his nature.

Now the woman was faced by the only man who had no sin – Jesus. Would he throw the first stone? No, of course not. Because only sinners throw stones of condemnation at other sinners. That's why the world is in such a mess – with one lot of sinners endlessly attacking another lot of sinners, and the other lot endlessly retaliating. And the only one who can see the way though the mess is the sinless one who was himself to be put to death by sinners. When he asked the woman if there was anyone left to condemn her, she said, 'No one, Lord.' And she was right, because the Lord said to her, 'Neither do I condemn you. Go, and sin no more.' And that is what he says to all sinners.

Such is his amazing grace!

Day 5: The First Sunday in Lent
The temptations

Matthew 4:1-11; Mark 1:9-15; Luke 4:1-13

Jesus was led by the Spirit into the desert, where he fasted for forty days and nights, and was tempted by the devil, who used quotations from Scripture. He was tempted to turn stones into bread, to throw himself from the top of the Temple and to worship the devil in return for all the kingdoms of the world. He rejected all three temptations with his own quotations from Scripture, and the devil left him.

Whoever the devil might be, it is comforting to know that we are not the only ones to have heard his insidious whispers, and that Jesus had temptations just as we do, but he also rejected them. This shows it can be done, though we tend to think it was easier for him than for us. But we are probably wrong. Experience tells us that the forces of evil gain in strength in proportion to the good they wish to destroy. The greater the good, the greater the evil ranged against it. So how did Jesus manage to reject temptations to evil? What was his secret?

I think it was that he had something in his life, his mind, his heart which was more important to him than anything the devil had to offer him, something that he wasn't prepared to sacrifice for anything else in the world. I'll expand on what that meant for Jesus in a moment, but it also applies to us in dealing with *our* temptations. We can overcome them if we realise there are things in our lives that are more important to us than the momentary satisfaction of giving in to temptation – for example, our health, our families and relationships, our reputation, our conscience, our principles. Thousands of people overcome temptation every day because of things like these, which they know aren't worth sacrificing for what their temptation offers. That is how alcoholics and drug addicts triumph over their addictions, how husbands and wives remain faithful, how treasurers refuse to fiddle the books, how politicians avoid telling lies, how people refuse to accept or offer bribes. I'm not saying it's easy. Sometimes the pressure of temptation is so great that it makes us forget what we will lose if we give in to it. That is why we need to be sure what is most important to us *before* temptation comes; then we are less likely to forget it.

The most important thing in Jesus' life was his relationship with God. And he never forgot it. We can see it clearly in the three quotations he used to reject the devil's temptations: (1) 'You shall not live on bread alone, but on every word that comes from the mouth of God'; (2) 'You shall not test the Lord your God'; (3) 'You shall bow down to the Lord your God, and serve him alone.' All of them put God first, and that is what Jesus did all his life.

I only have space here to look at the first of those quotations in more detail: 'You shall not live on bread alone, but on every word that comes from the mouth of God.' Many people who don't believe in God would agree with the first half of that statement but not the second. The world of commerce and advertising certainly realises that we have other needs to satisfy than our need for bread alone. For instance, we need beauty, relaxation, excitement, information and entertainment, and there are whole industries devoted to satisfying those needs. We do have a strong bodily need for food but we also have a hunger for life in all its fullness.

Those who believe in God share in all these needs but they also have a hunger for God. Jesus certainly had a hunger for God, and he knew the devil had nothing to offer him which could compare with the satisfaction of living 'on every word that comes from the mouth of God'.

When a lawyer asked Jesus what he should do 'to gain eternal life' (Luke 10:25), Jesus didn't tell him to join a yoga class, listen to Classic FM, read a good book, take more exercise or even watch *Songs of Praise*; he directed him to the words of God written in the Law: 'You shall love the Lord your God with all your heart, and with all your soul, and with all your strength, and with all your mind; and your neighbour as yourself,' and told him 'Do this, and you will live.' And that's the best way of all to defeat the devil.

Day 6: Monday
Who knows best?

Genesis 2:15-17

God gives Man the task of looking after the Garden of Eden and says he can eat from any of the trees except from the Tree of Knowledge, because he would die.

The first chapter of Genesis gives a wonderful picture of a perfect creation. Everything comes into being in response to the command of God and takes its place in an orderly system which God declares to be very good. This happy feeling continues in the second creation story in chapter 2 with the creation of Man and the wonderful environment of the Garden of Eden for him to live and work in as God's estate manager. There is only one small limitation on his freedom. He must not eat from the Tree of Knowledge or he will die. However, Man (or Adam – it's the same word in Hebrew) doesn't question the prohibition at the time and helps God to find an equal partner for him by naming the animals as they are created and then delighting in the creation of Woman.

Genesis 3:1-7

The serpent persuades the Woman to try the fruit from the Tree of Knowledge, and she gives some to her husband to eat as well. They both become ashamed of their nakedness and cover it up.

We could see this coming, of course, from the moment when the Lord God announced the prohibition. The Serpent, like a skilled salesman, only needed to draw the Woman's attention to the tree and describe its wonderful powers, to make her want its fruit. God's command seemed to be an unnecessary limitation on their freedom, maybe a sign that God wanted to keep them under his thumb.

The full name of the Tree was 'The Tree of the Knowledge of Good and Evil' but its meaning is obscure. 'The Knowledge of Good and Evil' could mean the knowledge of right and wrong in a moral sense, or the knowledge of what is beneficial and what is harmful in a more general sense. Or it could mean the knowledge of everything, because 'good and evil' was a Hebrew idiom for 'everything'. In the context of the story it could mean sexual knowledge, because after they'd eaten the fruit the Man and the Woman became ashamed of their nakedness, whereas they hadn't been before (2:25). But presumably sex was God's chosen way of reproduction and they would have come to know about that without eating fruit from a tree. So why should God want to keep this knowledge from them, whatever it was?

By asking such questions we may be missing the point and doing exactly what the Serpent and the Woman and the Man did – thinking that we know better than God and that we don't need to obey him. So they disobeyed God's command because they resented anything that prevented them from doing what they wanted. The story reveals a basic flaw in human nature. We think we know best and don't like being told what to do by anybody else, even God.

Genesis 9:8-17

After the flood God establishes a new Covenant with Noah and all living creatures, that there will never be another flood which destroys all living things on earth – the sign of this Covenant is the rainbow.

Adam and Eve's flawed nature was soon passed on to future generations. Their son, Cain, murdered his younger brother, Abel (Genesis 4:8); and before we know where we are the whole world is full of violence (6:11). But God didn't give up on his creation altogether; he decided to make a clean start, but saved Noah, his family and a whole zoo of animals so that life could go on.

After the flood he made a Covenant with the survivors and all future generations, that there would never be such a worldwide flood again. He was determined to make his creation succeed.

The sign of the promise is the rainbow – beautiful but evanescent. Can we rely on it? God has given us a great deal of freedom in running the world, despite our sin. But if it came to the point where we were in danger of destroying it completely, would he leave us to it? We can only hope that he will give us sufficient nudges in the right direction long before we arrive at the zero hour of total destruction. The question, then, is this: will we heed those nudges? Or will we insist on going on our disobedient way – because we still think we know best?

Day 7: Tuesday
Confession

Psalm 32

The Psalmist describes his misery when he concealed his guilt and did not admit his sin, and the blessed relief that came to him when he confessed and was forgiven. He commends others to do the same and also to turn to God for help in time of trouble. He will show them the way to go and, unlike the wicked, they will shout for joy.

When something is preying on your mind, such as guilt or regret for something you've done, or you're worrying about things going on in your life, don't try to bottle it up so that it wakes you in the middle of the night. Otherwise it will completely drain your energy, your powers of concentration and your happiness. Instead, read this Psalm, and then confess your guilt and anxieties to God (and to anyone else who needs to know – but not to all and sundry).

The longer you put it off, the worse it will get. The worst of all is when you're so successful in hiding your dark secrets from others that you think they've gone away – in fact, you deny that they were ever there. But they haven't gone away. They're still lurking in the cellar of your mind waiting to burst up to the surface with devastating force at times of unexpected pressure.

God is always wanting to forgive, but we can't receive his forgiveness until we admit our need for it. There are many times in our lives when we need to say 'Sorry' to people – from bumping into them in the street to letting them down when they were relying on us. If we do say 'Sorry' we're often forgiven, but if we don't, we aren't because people will think that we don't care, and *they* won't care much for *us* either. God wants to forgive – so say 'Sorry' to him more often. The joy of forgiveness is something that has to be experienced to be believed. It's a joy like no other. It's a weight off the mind and the healing of a pain in the heart (and very often involves physical healing as well).

God is also waiting to help, but we can't experience his help until we ask for it. In our daily lives we know that asking is a dynamic action. It makes things happen that wouldn't happen otherwise. We can stand in the fast food queue all day but we know we'll get a hamburger only if we ask for it. We can get lost and wander around the wrong part of town for hours but we know that if we stop to ask we're likely to be pointed in the right direction eventually. But when it comes to our relationship with God we are sometimes too reluctant and (we think) sophisticated to ask for help. All I can say to that is this: try it and find out for yourself. God will not always give you what you want, but he will give you what you need, and that's far more important.

Psalm 25:1-10

The Psalmist trusts that God will protect him from those who wish to humiliate and discredit him and asks God to show him the right way to go. He asks forgiveness for past sins and casts himself on God's constant love. God is good and leads those who obey him in right paths.

There can't be many people who really don't care what others think about them. Those who *are* like that must have such a high opinion of themselves that they think they are above criticism, or they have reached such a low state of mind that they don't care about anything any more and even despise themselves. But, for most of us, what other people think of us is important for our self-respect and also helps us to avoid behaving in unacceptable ways. Of course, we can take our neighbours' opinions *too* seriously and abandon our individuality in order to do and be what we think *others* think is right. Worse still, we might cover up our faults and pretend to be what we aren't.

We don't know the details of the Psalmist's situation, but he may have had some guilty secrets – the sins of his youth (verse 7) which he didn't want his enemies to expose (verse 2). And, in the second half of the Psalm, he confesses them to God and asks for forgiveness (verses 11, 16-20). This made me think of the anguish of those politicians and celebrities in modern times whose sins are exposed very publicly in the press. The tabloids, especially, often reveal the shortcomings of people in the public eye, sometimes justifiably and sometimes not, while we sit back and read about it, feeling superior now that their wild oats have come home to roost (to mix metaphors). But I wonder what it feels like to be in their shoes? Perhaps Psalm 25 can give us a clue.

Day 8: Wednesday
Justification

Romans 5:12-19

Sin and death have spread to the whole human race from the first man, Adam. This happened even before the Law began to take account of sin. But the free gift of God's grace is better than that: it also began with one Man, Jesus Christ, but far from bringing death to everyone, God's grace brings justification to those who receive it, so that through the obedience of that one Man, Jesus, many will live and reign with him. For as by one man's disobedience many became sinners, so by one Man's obedience many will become righteous.

It's not always easy to understand what Paul is talking about when he uses words like justify, justified and justification in his letters, even though we still use them in everyday speech. When we say, for instance, that something is justified we mean that it is right and can be shown to be right. If I chop down a tree because it is rotten and in danger of falling on my house, I can claim that I am justified. It's not easy to justify certain actions, especially political decisions, but at least we know what it means when we use the word.

The problem is that Paul seems to use the word in an odd way which contradicts normal usage. What he says is that God justifies the sinner. This is a contradiction in terms because it is saying that the one who has done wrong is regarded as being in the right. It is a startling way of describing God's grace. It seems contrary to natural justice. In the parable of the Pharisee and the tax collector praying in the Temple (Luke 18:1-14), it was the sinful, penitent tax collector who 'went back home justified', said Jesus, not the proud Pharisee who was meticulous in keeping the Law.

A young soldier deserted from Napoleon's army in the height of battle and was afterwards arrested and ordered to be shot. His mother went to Napoleon to plead for mercy, but Napoleon said that the soldier didn't deserve mercy. The mother pointed out that if he deserved it, it wouldn't be mercy; it would be justice. Napoleon relented and issued a pardon.

We should be glad that God's mercy is offered to those who don't deserve it. He forgives our sins without first weighing them against our good deeds, if we have any. His forgiveness is free and unconditional, except that we have to accept it before we can benefit from it. It truly is the 'amazing grace' that John Newton wrote about in his famous hymn. He wrote about it because he had experienced it for himself and it changed his life.

Romans 10:8b-13

The Good News is that it is by faith that you are justified – believing in your heart that Jesus is Lord and has been raised from the dead. This applies to everyone, both Jew and Gentile, because everyone who cries out to the Lord for help will be saved.

Leading up to this passage, Paul has done something very radical – he has quoted from the Book of Deuteronomy (30:11-14) and turned its meaning upside down, just as he turned the common meaning of 'justification' upside down in Romans 5 above. Deuteronomy says quite clearly that it is by obeying God's commandments that the people will live, and Paul recognises that in his letter (10:5). He then goes on to say, however, that it is not by obeying God's Law but by faith that we are put right with God, or 'justified' (10:10). This is the famous doctrine of 'justification by faith' which was so central to Paul's interpretation of the gospel.

In a sense, both Deuteronomy and Paul are right. Deuteronomy is right because we can only really live as individuals and as communities if we put into practice the principles of God's moral Law, but Paul is right because we make such a mess of trying to obey God's Law that we need constantly to be forgiven (and to forgive one another) in order to make any progress. It is only by the free grace of God that we can keep going at all. If God started practising strict justice only, we would get nowhere. What we need is mercy.

Day 9: Thursday
Matters of life and death

1 Peter 3:18-22

Christ suffered for sins once and for all, the just for the unjust, in order to bring us to God. Having suffered a physical death he was made alive by the Spirit and went and preached to the spirits in prison who had disobeyed in the days of Noah while God was preparing the ark in which to save Noah and his family on the water. Likewise, the water of baptism now saves you, not by washing your bodies but by the appeal to God of the good conscience of Jesus Christ, now raised from the dead and seated at God's right hand in heaven, to rule over all angels, authorities and powers.

It is one of the paradoxes of human life that it is the just who suffer for the unjust and not the other way round. As judge Baron Bowen of Colwood put it:

> The rain it raineth on the just
> and also on the unjust fella:
> but chiefly on the just, because
> the unjust steals the just's umbrella.

That's a comical way of illustrating a very serious law of life. We try to correct it by sending the unjust to prison, but ultimately the victim of crime usually suffers more than the criminal, even when the criminal is punished. So the Just Man, Jesus Christ, submitted himself to this unwritten law of life when he died on the cross for the sin of the world – the just for the unjust. It was an outrage against justice, but it was the only possible way of showing mercy. He was treated like a criminal and died the death of a criminal in order that we sinners might be treated like the children of God. The driving force behind his death was the love of God for all the world. And that love extends even to those who have died. That is illustrated in Peter's letter by the reference to Christ, who, having himself passed through the waters of death, preached to those imprisoned in the underworld, who had drowned in the Flood. God wants everyone to be able to respond to his love, both the living and the dead.

Those who do respond here on earth are usually baptised, and baptism, especially in the form of total immersion, symbolises death and resurrection as the baptised are plunged under the water and rise again to begin a new life in the Spirit. And this is possible because, first of all, Jesus passed through the waters of death and rose again to life.

So we are called to share in Christ's resurrection by first sharing in his death. Paul makes this clear in Romans 6:1-11. But what does this mean? Not just that we have to die physically but that we have to learn how to die to sin and self in this life. Let me illustrate what dying to self might mean from the life of George Muller. He was a nineteenth-century Brethren pastor and evangelist in Bristol, who decided not to ask for financial support for his work but to trust in God to provide, in answer to prayer. In this way he was able to build a large complex of homes for the care of poor and homeless children at Ashley Down, just outside Bristol. When he was asked what was the secret of his spiritual life, he said, 'There was once a day when I died; utterly died – died to George Muller, his opinions, preferences, tastes and will; died to the world, its approval or censure; died to the approval or blame even of my brethren and friends, and, since then, I have studied only to show myself approved unto God.'

Most of us never reach that level of self-giving, but if we keep on following Christ every day, we will discover the truth that it is only as we die that we can rise again. Life and death are closely bound together. Some of the richest experiences of our lives come to us when we forget ourselves – die to ourselves. At one end of the scale that might simply be when we lose ourselves in a book or a piece of music, or it might be when we fall in love or hold a baby in our arms, or give all our attention to creating a work of art. At the other end of the scale it will be when we give ourselves gladly to a cause that is bigger than ourselves. And all such experiences prepare us for the ultimate realisation that the resurrection life means losing ourselves in God and knowing that nothing else matters but him – and yet knowing also that because of him everything matters, even ourselves.

Day 10: Friday
Spring harvest

Deuteronomy 26:1-11

When the Israelites settle in Canaan each one of them is instructed to take the first fruits of their harvest in a basket to the holy place of worship. They should give it to the priest, who will place it before the altar. It is a sign that they have entered the land which God had promised them; and each one shall recall their nation's history – how God released them from slavery in Egypt and brought them to the land flowing with milk and honey. They shall worship the Lord, rejoicing in all that he has done for them. And the Levites, and the foreigners who live among them, shall share in the celebration.

All modern harvest festivals are rooted in the past, recalling generations of thankfulness for the good things of the earth and for the faithfulness of God. We should remember our spiritual forebears entering the Promised Land and bringing harvest gifts to acknowledge their dependence on the Living God. Or we could remember the Pilgrim Fathers, celebrating their first harvest in a New World with the help of the native people.

I look back to my boyhood and remember churches adorned in joyful praise with flowers and fruit and vegetable pride, and hearty voices singing, 'Come ye thankful people come', while choirs enthusiastically proclaimed, 'The heavens are telling the glory of God'. Perhaps they remembered then the wartime harvests of 'Dig for Victory' days, and land girls and rationing, and the bloodier harvest of battlefields, and city streets, and smoke-filled skies and unforgiving seas.

And today we cannot forget the failed harvests of Africa, which moved us for a while to sing, 'Feed the World'. For even the harvests that are lost to drought and flood and storm announce our dependence on our God. Life is rich, but fragile, on this earth of good and ill, and every harvest lost to war and greed makes clear how much we need the world community's good will.

So when we join in harvest song again this year, let us look back with thankfulness for that great chain of life in which we share, and God's provision for our earthly good. But may we never forget to look around and see the ones who long to share that earthly good with you and me but are unable to do so, for a multitude of cleverly argued but unpersuasive reasons.

It may seem strange to have a reading about harvest in the middle of Lent. Isn't Lent about fasting and deserts rather than feasting and fruitful fields? Yes, but there is a direct link between Lent and Harvest, nevertheless. Lent overlaps the end of winter and the beginning of spring, and the word 'lenten' derives from the Anglo-Saxon for lengthen, which referred to the lengthening daylight of February, March and April. Lent is therefore associated with the season of planting and sowing which eventually leads to the harvest, of course.

For harvest is not a sudden miracle. It grows out of weedy, stony ground, which has the God-given potential to bear fruit, but the ground needs to be prepared and sown, and the growth tended, before the harvest can come. So it is with Lent, when we prepare the ground of our hearts with the plough of repentance, and clear it of stones and weeds. Then we can plant fresh seeds of devotion and commitment to God, and look forward with faith and hope to the harvest of the Spirit in days to come. For the spiritual life is about growing up and bearing fruit (Ephesians 4:15; Philippians 3:14; Galatians 5:22, 23). And Lent is the season when we tidy up our spiritual gardens to make room for new growth. Lent may often seem to be a time of misery and despair, as we set about the back-breaking (and heartbreaking) work of dealing with our sins, but if we do that work properly, it should also be a season of hope and joy because of the new life ahead.

Day 11: Saturday
Protection

Psalm 91:1, 2, 9-16

If you shelter in God, and say, 'The Lord is my refuge. I will trust in him,' no evil shall come near you, for he will call on his angels to hold you up, lest you fall, and he will protect you from lions and snakes. (God says,) 'I will save and protect the one who loves me and knows my name. Whoever calls to me I will answer, and I will be with them in trouble. I will rescue them and honour them. I will give them long life and the knowledge that they are safe in me.'

This is a puzzling Psalm because it seems to offer those who trust in God insurance against trouble – something that we have long believed was not God's policy. What should make us especially wary of the Psalm is that the devil tempted Jesus by quoting from it (verses 11 and 12 – see Matthew 4:6 and Luke 4:11, 12). The temptation was to throw himself from the pinnacle of the temple, relying on angels to give him a safe landing. Jesus answered the devil with another quotation: 'You shall not tempt the Lord your God.' It was obvious that a leap from the Temple would serve no useful purpose in his mission, even if angels did help him out. It would give people an entirely wrong impression of what he had come to do – not spectacular demonstrations of supernatural power that did nobody any good, but a life of service and sacrifice out of love for a sinful world.

In rejecting the devil, however, Jesus didn't dismiss the idea that God can protect people from danger. But it wasn't his chosen way of doing things. There are many examples in religious history of the kind of protection spoken of by the Psalmist, when people have called on God's help in desperate circumstances and found it was given to them in unusual ways. For instance, the time when Gladys Aylward was sent into a Chinese prison to calm down a prisoner who was running amok with an axe and attacking everybody in sight. She boldly confronted him and persuaded him to hand over the axe. Such courage can have amazing effects on adversaries, as well as giving people the ability to face situations where they would normally consider such action foolhardy. There is such an example in Israel's history, when David, the shepherd boy, offered to use the shepherding skills he'd learned in driving off lions and bears, in order to defeat the Philistine giant, Goliath.

On the other hand, many people have thrown themselves into the sea to rescue someone in trouble, and not all of them have survived. It would be churlish to say that those who drowned didn't trust in God. The truth probably is that those who act bravely and survive do so whether they trust in God or not – and the same could be said of those who don't survive. Trusting in God for protection will give us strength, but only God knows how it will all work out. One thing we can be sure of: he doesn't run a protection racket.

And that is why we need to be wary of this Psalm. It can give false expectations to those who are only interested in supernatural power, and their delusions can lead others astray as well – perhaps with tragic results. But it can give strength and courage to those who genuinely love and trust God and only seek to do his will. They will then regard troubles and dangers as occupational hazards, just like St Paul who said, 'I have learned to be content in whatever situation I find myself . . . I can face any circumstances through the one who strengthens me' (Philippians 4:11, 13). He knew, as all Christians should know, that following Jesus involves carrying a cross. And all the martyrs, ancient and modern, can bear witness to that.

Day 12: The Second Sunday in Lent
Nicodemus

John 3:1-17

Nicodemus has a private meeting with Jesus at night. Jesus talks to him about the kingdom of God, the new birth, the working of the Spirit, and the heavenly Son of Man who must be 'lifted up' like Moses' bronze serpent in the wilderness. But Nicodemus doesn't understand a single word. Jesus tells him that God loved the world so much he didn't want to destroy it but to save it, by giving his only Son, so that whoever believes in him will have new life.

Nicodemus thought
that because Jesus did signs and wonders
he must be a man of God.
But Jesus knew
that even the devil does signs and wonders
and deceives the world with them;
but the true Man of God
seeks only to do God's will.
And that is something the devil can never do.

Nicodemus thought
that the kingdom of God was a theocratic state
that would be entered by triumphant processions
of shouting zealots.
But Jesus knew
that God's kingdom cannot even be seen,
let alone entered,
except by those who have been reborn
to a new kind of life.

Nicodemus thought
that being born again
meant re-entering his mother's womb.
(Did he laugh when he said that?)
But Jesus knew
that being born again meant not baby bodies
but new hearts and minds,
fashioned by the washing of repentance
and the breathing of the Spirit.

'And the Son of Man,' said Jesus,
'must be lifted up on a stick
like Moses' serpent in the wilderness[1]
that everyone might see
how much God loved the world,
and, seeing, live.'
We aren't told
what Nicodemus made of that.

But was he any wiser,
when he came with spices
to lay the body of Jesus to rest
in the tomb?[2]
And did he ever meet those
who later found the tomb
empty?

Do we too, like Nicodemus,
misunderstand
when Jesus speaks of heavenly things
in the earthly language of metaphor and parable?
How, then, shall we ever understand him
when he speaks the language of heaven
in a body raised from the dead?

---

1 See not only Numbers 21:8, 9 but John 12:32, 33.   2 See John 19:39, 40.

Day 13: Monday
Abraham

Genesis 12:1-4a

The Lord told Abram to leave his father's home and go to a land which the Lord would show him, where he would become a great nation. God's blessing would extend from Abram to the whole human family.

Genesis 15:1-12, 17, 18

The Lord appeared to Abram in a vision; and Abram asked him who would inherit his possessions, seeing that he had no offspring of his own. The Lord promised that Abram would have a son and that his descendants would be as many as the stars in heaven. Abram believed God, who then repeated his promise of the land and told Abram to offer a sacrifice. Then he fell into a deep sleep and saw a vision in which God established a Covenant with him, giving the Promised Land to him and his descendants.

Genesis 17:1-7, 15, 16

The Lord appeared to Abram again and renewed his Covenant with him. He also changed his name to Abraham (father of a multitude). He also changed Abraham's wife's name from Sarai to Sarah (princess) and promised that she would bear Abraham a son and become a mother of nations.

God has made a universe which is constantly changing as he works out his purposes for his creation. The changes in human history are also signs of God at work as he leads us towards the fulfilment of his vision of the unity of all things in Christ (Ephesians 1:10). The changes which take place in our lives are all part of this greater plan, even though we cannot always see it. The God who makes all things new is inevitably a God of change and growth, not of static calm. We may not always like this, but it is the way things are, and we have to try and view it positively. But because of our limited human vision we tend to regard change as threatening, and in depressed moods we sing with Henry Francis Lyte, 'Change and decay in all around I see'.[1] Yet in a different mood Lyte might have written, 'Change and *growth* in all around I see', because every change which comes along, even though it may seem to us to be painful and damaging, is an opportunity for something new. But we can only see that opportunity by faith. As Paul said, 'We walk by faith and not by sight' (2 Corinthians 5:7).

The story of Abraham's faith journey can throw light on our own faith journeys. Like our journeys, it was full of twists and turns. He didn't always give the impression that he knew where he was going or what he was doing. Sometimes his travels took him to dangerous places and he had to turn back on his tracks. He gave away the whole of the Jordan valley (a hefty chunk of the land of Canaan) to his nephew, Lot. Even when he seemed to have arrived in the Promised Land he passed on through it to Egypt because of a famine. He fought battles and confronted kings, but in everything he kept his faith in God.

So Abraham's journey was not an easy one. Nor can we expect our faith journeys to be any easier. What we can learn from Abraham is that whatever happens we should keep on going, one step at a time, trusting in the God who knows the way and keeps his promises, even when they seem impossible. And what made Abraham's personal journey important was that it was part of God's bigger plan, which we as individuals can often lose sight of but need to believe in. Abraham was not just an individual but the head of a large community of family and servants, who travelled with him – the people of God in embryo. We are his spiritual descendants because we are members of that family too. We don't travel to the Promised Land alone but in the company of many others. The kingdom of God is not a private reward but a communal gift.

---

1 From the hymn 'Abide with me'.

Day 14: Tuesday
Trust in God

Psalm 121

I look up to the hills for help, but help comes from the Lord of all creation. He is always awake to protect you. He never sleeps. He will always keep you safe from evil.

This Psalmist is absolutely certain that God neither slumbers nor sleeps; and he's surely right. A sleeping god (like Baal on Mount Carmel – 1 Kings 18:27) is worse than no god at all because you don't put your trust in no god, but you might rely on a sleeping one and be let down.

A certain bishop was lying awake worrying one night when he heard God speaking to him. 'You go to sleep, bishop. *I'll* stay awake for the rest of the night.' And, of course, God *doesn't* sleep, though not everybody has believed that, not even all psalmists (for example, Psalm 44:23). God does some of his best work while we sleep (see Psalm 127:2). Have you ever gone to bed with a problem and woken up next morning knowing how to solve it? The whole universe manages to keep going without us having to stay awake worrying about the details; we can safely let God do that.

When Bishop Ridley was condemned to be burnt at the stake in 1555, his brother came to see him on the day before the execution and offered to stay with him through the night. But Ridley declined the offer, saying, 'No, no, that you shall not, for I mind, God willing, to go to bed and to sleep as quietly tonight as ever I did in my life.'

It must be wonderful to have such a confident faith. Some might call it naïve but it is nearer the truth than those who question it. When she was 81 Thora Hird, when asked about her faith in God said, 'I've never really had to look for God, because I've always been sure he is there. He doesn't desert us – we desert him.' Although the experience of Jesus on the cross – when he felt that

38

God had abandoned him – seems to contradict that, I don't think it does. When we think that God has deserted us, it simply means that we no longer feel his presence, for God was as near to Jesus on Calvary as he had been at any other time in his life.

Psalm 22:23-31

Praise the Lord, all you people of God, because he remembers the poor in their suffering and answers their cries for help. I will praise him and make my vows to him, among the worshipping congregation. All nations and races will turn to the Lord and worship him, for he is the universal King. The proud will bow down to him, and future generations will serve him when they learn how he saved his people.

We are more familiar with the beginning of this Psalm than the ending, because Jesus quoted the opening words as he hung on the cross: 'My God, my God, why have you forsaken me?' This shows that Jesus was truly human. As he was dying, he felt both physical pain and spiritual anguish. But, worst of all, he felt that God had deserted him. The Psalm then describes the agony of a man under attack from vicious enemies, and as we read it we can't help but compare it with Jesus' crucifixion. Yet the end of the Psalm is a shout of triumphant praise, as if to show that God's victories are won in the midst of and by means of suffering, not least the un-deserved suffering of the Son of God for the sins of the whole world.

Psalm 27

The Psalmist begins with a bold confidence in God's ability to protect him from his enemies, but his confidence wavers as he cries out to God for help. In the end he realises that he just has to be brave and trust in the Lord.

Many of us have experienced the Psalmist's wavering between confidence and despair which tends to take over our lives in difficult times. But what relief we find when we learn how to let go and trust in God. 'He doesn't desert us; we desert him.'

Day 15: Wednesday
Salvation by grace

Romans 4:1-5, 13-25

Paul argues that God accepted Abraham not because of his obedience to the Law but because of his faith. God's promise to Abraham and his descendants that they would inherit the world wasn't made because they obeyed God's law but because they believed in God. Therefore the promise is based entirely on God's grace. Abraham believed God's promise that he would be the father of many nations, even though he was very old and his wife, Sarah, was barren. He believed that anything was possible with a God who can raise the dead and make something out of nothing; and because he didn't doubt God's promise, God accepted him as righteous. And we too will be accepted because we believe in him who died for our sins and was raised to make us right with God.

It's very easy for modern readers to lose patience with Paul when he is expounding an argument. His rabbinical method of interpreting the scriptures is so different from our own and his terminology often seems obscure and alien. In other words, we don't really understand what he is trying to say.

Sometimes it helps to read between the lines or look just below the surface of his words and unwrap his metaphors to get to his meaning. Take the name 'Abraham', for instance. For all Jews (like Paul) it conjures up the idea of family – the chosen family of God, of which Abraham was the human father and the Jews were his children (or descendants). Paul saw this family as expanding, thanks to Jesus, the Son of God (our elder brother), to include the Gentiles (the rest of humankind) because God had promised Abraham that he would be 'the father of many nations' (or races).

So the idea of God's family is the half-hidden background to what Paul is trying to say here, and though the secular modern world seems hell-bent (literally) on destroying the family, at least it is an idea which modern people should be able to understand. The head of the family is an ideal Father. (Many will have a problem with this because of absentee or abusive fathers and the omission of any reference to a Mother.) Nevertheless the ideal heavenly Father, whose nature is unconditional love, is at the heart of Paul's family metaphor.

We know the Father's love is unconditional because he is a God who forgives freely (a God of grace). He acquits the guilty; he regards the unrighteous as if they were in a right relationship with him (the righteous); those who are bad (unjust) he treats as if they were good (he justifies them). That is the nature of unconditional love, and it is the nature of God the Father. If we want to know what God's love is like, we could do worse than read Paul's description of love in 1 Corinthians 13:4-7. We should also look at Jesus: he forgave the soldiers who nailed him to the cross, and told the story of the father who welcomed his wastrel son home. When Paul boggles our minds with words like justification and righteousness he is simply talking about being loved by our heavenly Father.

'Faith' is another word which may confuse us when Paul uses it. (Does it mean 'belief' or 'trust' or both?) We can even get the idea that it is our faith which saves us. But Paul knew that faith, important as it is, is not the most fundamental thing of all; love is (1 Corinthians 13:13). God's love for us is basic. It is God's grace which 'saves' us (saves us from destroying ourselves by making a mess of our lives and restores us to a healthy relationship with him). We can't earn that or work for it. It is freely given. It is that love which embraces infants in Baptism and is publicly acknowledged by them later in Confirmation. It is the love which God has for the whole world, though the whole world doesn't realise it. Those who receive it by faith begin to live by it and learn to love God and their neighbours (some more quickly than others). But it is not their love for God and their neighbours which comes first but God's love for them, which has been revealed most clearly of all in the life, death and resurrection of Jesus Christ. God wants a loving family. That's why he called Abraham. It's why he sent Jesus. And it's why he calls you, me and all the world to be his children.

Day 16: Thursday
Unavoidable suffering

Mark 8:31-38

Jesus taught his disciples that the Son of Man must endure much suffering because he would be rejected by the religious authorities and be put to death, but after three days he would rise again. Peter started to protest but Jesus rebuked him. And he spoke to the crowd and his disciples and said, 'If anyone wants to come after me let them deny self, take up their cross and follow me; because whoever may want to save their life will lose it, but whoever may lose their life on account of me and the gospel will save it. For whoever is ashamed of me and my words, the Son of Man will also be ashamed of them, when he comes in the Father's glory.'

This is the turning point in Jesus' mission. No sooner has Peter told Jesus that he thinks he is the Messiah than Jesus speaks for the first time about the inevitable suffering and death which lie ahead of him, and makes it clear that those who follow him must also expect the same. Unlike Peter, we don't step forward to remonstrate with Jesus. We step back in fear and trembling. How can we follow him, then? It's too much to expect. And we know that when it came to the crunch, everybody stepped back, even Peter, and abandoned Jesus to his chosen fate. The only one to take up his cross and follow him was not a disciple but a conscript – Simon of Cyrene.

Jesus spoke plainly about his unavoidable sufferings and warned his disciples that they too should be prepared to face suffering if they were to follow him. When he challenged them to take up their own cross, they may have understood him to be speaking metaphorically, but they couldn't have guessed that the literal reality of his cross lay just around the corner.

Since then many have followed Jesus to the death, even Peter according to tradition. And in every generation many Christians have faced suffering and death because of their faithfulness to

Jesus and his gospel. One of the most famous in recent times was Oscar Romero, Archbishop of San Salvador, who was shot dead while celebrating Mass in a hospital chapel. His leading role in the struggle for social justice in El Salvador had brought him into conflict with the authorities. He knew that many of his priests had already been killed because of their stand for justice, and he had received many death threats himself, so he was aware of what might happen but accepted the dangers as the unavoidable consequence of his faithfulness to Christ.

Paul was present at the martyrdom of Stephen and he persecuted Christians himself before he was converted on the Damascus Road, so he obviously knew that being a Christian would not be a bed of roses. But he was proud 'to share in Christ's sufferings and become like him in his death' (Philippians 3:10), or, as he put it elsewhere, to 'bear on (his) body the marks of Jesus' (Galatians 6:17).

Faithfulness to the Lord Jesus is the key to our understanding of Jesus' words to those who follow him. It is clear that not all Christians will be called to martyrdom, or even be persecuted, though there are many who will. My own personal sufferings for Christ pale into insignificance alongside the sufferings of the martyrs, and, to be honest, most of my 'sufferings' have not been because I am a follower of Jesus – they have been the kind of sufferings which afflict most people during the course of their lives: bereavement, stress, sickness, anxiety, etc. I don't regard them as a cross which I've taken up for Jesus but as various burdens which he has helped me to bear.

However, such sufferings are relevant to my Christian discipleship if they become tests of my faithfulness by tempting me to give up my faith. I would like to think that I could be faithful to Christ in all circumstances, however hostile. But I can't be sure of that any more than the disciples could be. I can just seek to strengthen my bond with Jesus by faith and obedience day by day, and trust that I shall be ready for the time of testing when it comes.

Day 17: Friday
Citizens of heaven

Philippians 3:17–4:1

Paul calls on his fellow Christians to follow his example and not that of those who are enemies of the cross of Christ. Such people are heading for destruction because their god is their belly and they glory in their shame, having their minds on earthly things. But we are citizens of heaven, from which the Lord Jesus Christ will come and transform this lowly body to make it like his glorious body. And that is why the Christians should stand firm in the Lord.

Paul was not a man to mince his words, even when writing to his 'beloved' Philippians, his 'joy and crown', whom he missed so much. He warned them of those many 'enemies of the cross of Christ', whose god was their belly and who were heading for destruction. We can only guess whom Paul might have meant. Was it people in the Philippian Church or was it people in the world at large? It could have been either or both. But whoever these worshippers of the god of the belly were, their problem is strangely topical, not only because Lent is the season of fasting but because over-eating is increasingly recognised as a modern problem which is going to cause more and more health problems in the years ahead.

In fact, it's only one facet of the culture of self-indulgence which afflicts affluent societies everywhere – and Christians are influenced by it as much as anyone else because the culture of self-indulgence is so pervasive that we often fall under its spell without realising it. A new vicar was visiting one of his parishioners for the first time – a young mother with a young son. She wanted to impress the vicar with her piety and told him how she read the Bible every day (which she did). Then she turned to her little boy and said, 'William, go and fetch that big book that Mummy is always reading.' He went off and came back with a copy of a mail order catalogue.

The whole of the commercial world depends on self-indulgence for its success. Advertisers are constantly trying to persuade us to buy what they have to sell, whether we really need it or not. In fact, part of their aim is to create new 'wants' where they didn't exist before. In modern times, whole economic theories have been developed which regard 'greed' not as a vice but a virtue. If everybody suddenly stopped being greedy our economic system would probably collapse overnight – except that there is still plenty of genuine need in the world (especially the developing world) which commerce could meet if it set about it with a will, even though there might not be much immediate profit in it.

So the culture of over-indulgence has a powerful influence on all our lives, whether Christian or not. England may not be a nation of shopkeepers, as Napoleon claimed, but it is certainly becoming a nation of shopaholics. Even when the banks close down on Sundays and bank holidays, the shops stay open and thousands of people spend their time and money in them. Worse still, we all encourage our children and grandchildren to learn and accept commercial values. Young William would have had no difficulty in finding his mother's mail order catalogue because he would often have looked through it himself with a gleam in his eyes.

But Paul knew that Christians had a higher set of values to live by, which they had learned from Christ and his cross – not self-indulgence but self-giving, not greed but generosity, not superficial wants but deep needs. These are some of the higher values which we Christians are supposed to be living by. For, unlike belly worshippers, our minds are set on the values of heaven. Paul described Christians as 'citizens of heaven' who owed their allegiance to Christ as Lord, just as citizens of a Roman colony like Philippi owed their allegiance to the Emperor in Rome. And though the time was not far off when they would have to make a painful choice between those two loyalties, Paul is not contrasting them here but comparing them. What he is contrasting is the need for Christians to live by the values of heaven and not by the values of the world, and that is still very relevant to us today.

Day 18: Saturday
Unholy City, desecrated Temple

Luke 13:31-35

Some Pharisees warn Jesus to stay away from Jerusalem because Herod is plotting to kill him. But Jesus insists that he must go on with his mission until it has been completed. He must die in Jerusalem, even though he longed to gather its people to him. So the next time they saw him would be when the crowd welcomed him to Jerusalem with shouts of acclamation.

John 2:13-22

Jesus goes up to Jerusalem and drives out of the Temple those who were selling oxen and sheep and doves, and also the money changers, telling them not to make his Father's house a house of trade. His disciples remember that it was written, 'Zeal for your house has eaten me up', while others ask him what was the meaning of his actions. Jesus replies, 'Destroy this Temple, and in three days I will raise it up.' They think he is talking about the Temple building, but he means the Temple of his body. So when he was raised from the dead the disciples remembered this and believed the scripture and the things that Jesus said.

From his boyhood visits Jesus had loved Jerusalem and the Temple as the place where he had to be about his Father's business. And now he approaches them knowing that he is soon to finish his Father's business, not with a triumphal entry but by dying on a hill outside the city walls. According to prophecy, Jerusalem and the Temple were the spiritual centre of the world, to which all nations would eventually turn in their search for the God of Israel.

But now the city was ruled by hated foreigners, while the Temple was virtually closed to foreigners because of the corrupt market trading which occupied the Gentile Court. The Holy City and the Holy Temple were both desecrated. No wonder Jesus cried out in anguish as he travelled ever nearer to Jerusalem, because it had rejected his way of peace. Those early days in Galilee had seemed so promising, as the crowds gathered round him for healing and for truth. But now the religious authorities are seeking to end his mission. Jerusalem is their headquarters, where they hatch their murderous plots and send out spies to trap him. But Jesus did not waver from his course, despite the warnings from (friendly?) Pharisees to stay away because Herod was plotting to kill him. Instead of seeing Jerusalem as a holy city, Jesus now saw it as the place where prophets die.

Likewise, the Temple had become the place where religion died – choked by corruption, greed and rigid authority. It was not a place where the people could worship the Father in spirit and in truth (John 4:21-24). The system of animal sacrifice was kept going by an elite who had a vested interest in it, and though we don't know what Jesus thought about that system, by his own death he was going to abolish it at a stroke, and the Romans would do the rest by destroying the Temple (and the city) 40 years later. But for the time being he could at least demonstrate his anger at the corrupt trading which operated in support of the sacrificial system (and of those who ran it), by fulfilling the prophecy of Malachi (3:1-4).

Some suggest that what Jesus did when he drove out the Temple traders is a sanction for all those who wish to use violence in a just cause. The weakness in that argument is that Jesus' use of violence was strictly limited. No one was badly injured or killed on that occasion (as far as we know), and it was a one-off example of righteous anger, not part of a long-term policy of violence. On other occasions, Jesus rejected violence completely. Violence against 'evil' powers may be justified from time to time but it is not justified by this event. Ultimately, Jesus followed his own teaching and loved his enemies to the very end, without resorting to the sword.

We might well ask what Jesus would think and do if he were to enter our own cities and temples. Are we an exclusive people unwilling to welcome strangers and only seeking to preserve our vested interests and our traditional ways and customs, or do we open our doors and our hearts to everyone?

Day 19: The Third Sunday in Lent
Water and spirit

John 4:5-42

Jesus meets a Samaritan woman beside Jacob's well and asks her for a drink. They get into conversation about springs and water, which the woman only partially understands. Jesus moves on to the subject of her personal life and she, thinking he must be a prophet, diverts him on to the religious questions which divide Jews and Samaritans. Jesus points out the nature of true worship and she is prompted to speak of the coming of the Messiah who knows everything. Jesus announces that he is the Messiah. The disciples return from the town where they'd gone for food and are surprised to find Jesus talking to a woman but they don't question him about it. The woman leaves her water jar and rushes off to the town to tell the people to come and see a man who might be the Messiah. Meanwhile the disciples are inviting Jesus to eat. Jesus tells them he has some food which they don't know about – and that is to do the will of God and complete his mission. He says the fields are ready for harvest, but he is speaking of the spiritual harvest waiting to be reaped. The Samaritans arrive from the town and ask Jesus to stay with them. So he stays for two days, and many believe his words and know him to be the Saviour of the World. Then Jesus returns to Galilee, saying that a prophet is not honoured in his own country. But many Galileans welcome him because they had been at the feast in Jerusalem and seen what he did there.

The Samaritan woman came to Jacob's well to draw water but she never did draw that water because she found one greater than Jacob there, who gave her a hope and a faith more refreshing than water. That is why, when she went off to tell her neighbours about Jesus, she left her bucket behind.

There are momentous times in our lives when we meet someone, or experience something, which stir the depths of our being and remind us that there is more to life than the humdrum tasks of daily existence. The springs of the Spirit of God within us are opened and life suddenly seems richer, more meaningful, more exhilarating and joyful. Such moments are often the turning points in our lives, and they release a flow of spiritual energy that continues with us through the years ahead – 'a spring of water bubbling up into life eternal.'

We don't know what happened to the Samaritan woman. No doubt she was back at the well the next day to draw water as usual, and yet surely life would never be the same again for her because of that meeting with Jesus.

The fact that she was a Samaritan and not a Jew should encourage us to believe what Jesus himself believed, that the good news of God's love is not for a chosen few but for all humankind. Everyone needs water in order to survive physically, but everyone needs more than water to live to the full.

In a world where every other person, it seems, wants to be a pop idol or a sports star or a celebrity of some kind or other, it is easy to wonder whether anyone has any higher ambitions than those of fame and fortune. But that would be too cynical because every human being has (potentially at least) deeper spiritual longings than these. Many long for a satisfying relationship. Many want to be good parents to their children. Some want to be of service to the community. Some want to add to the sum of human knowledge. Some want to create something beautiful or useful or inspiring. Some want to work for a worthy cause or devote themselves to a great ideal. Some want to please God by being better people. And just about everybody would like a little bit of happiness before they die. Such is the varied nature of human longings, the spiritual thirst for a deeper satisfaction than fame and fortune can provide.

And this story of the woman at the well serves to remind us that the true source of that deeper satisfaction lies in the Spirit of God himself. For when Jesus spoke to her about water he was really speaking about the Holy Spirit (John makes this clear in another place – John 7:37-39). Other things may bring us partial satisfaction in this world, but only the Spirit of God can fill the soul to overflowing.

Day 20: Monday
Water and rock

Exodus 17:1-7

The people of Israel journey through the wilderness and camp at Rephidim, where they find no water. So they blame Moses and demand that he gives them some, even threatening to stone him. Moses cries out to the Lord, asking what he can do with these complaining people. The Lord tells him to take the rod with which he struck the Nile and use it to strike a rock on Mount Horeb (Sinai). When he does so, water pours out of the rock and the people drink. But Moses names the place 'testing' and 'complaining', because the people tested God's power and complained at his absence.

Exodus 20:1-17

Moses tells the people the ten words (or commandments) which God had spoken to him on Mount Sinai, and which they are to obey.

During their time in the wilderness the Israelites had to learn many lessons, and one of them was their dependence on God every step of the way. It was God who had brought them out of slavery in Egypt and it was God who was leading them to the Promised Land. So they needed to trust God. But over and over again they failed to do so. Whenever anything went wrong they immediately started to grumble, even to the point of believing they'd been better off in Egypt (Exodus 16:3). So when they were hungry God gave them quails and manna to eat, and when they were thirsty he gave them water from the rock, to remind them of their dependence on him for everything.

This is a lesson we only seem to learn in times of hardship and deprivation (and not always then). At other times we tend to take everything for granted and congratulate ourselves on being in total control. Supermarkets give us the impression that food and drink will always be there for the asking, and we soon grumble if the particular item we're looking for is not on the shelves. Many people in the world, however, do not enjoy such luxury – and yet how often do we find that they are the ones who are most grateful for what they have? The people of Africa are more ready to praise God with joyful singing than the people of Britain.

The Book of Deuteronomy asserts that we do not live by bread alone (or water, for that matter) but we live by everything 'that comes from the mouth of the Lord' (Deuteronomy 8:3), and we remember that Jesus quoted those words when he was tempted by the devil to turn stones into bread. It is the words that God speaks to us that enable us to live. If we ignore them, our lives begin to suffer from malnutrition. If we ignore the ten commandments, for instance, society falls into chaos and anarchy. If we reject the way of Jesus, the Word of God and the true Bread from heaven, we are ill at ease with ourselves and with our neighbours. If we neglect the living water of the Spirit of God, our own spirits become dehydrated and shrivelled up, and we bear no fruit (see Galatians 5:22-23).

So Moses struck the rock on Mount Horeb (another name for Mount Sinai), and water came from it to quench the people's thirst, but later he met with God on Mount Sinai and received the commands which would help the people to live together – a living stream of wisdom and truth which still nourishes our society today and is still the foundation of our moral relationships. If we build our civilisation on the sand of lesser values, it will collapse; but the commandments of God were carved in stone and were meant to last.

Day 21: Tuesday
God's invitation

Isaiah 55:1-9

The Lord invites the exiles in Babylon to return to Jerusalem, which will be rebuilt on foundations of peace and justice, so that they can share in its new-found prosperity. The kingdom of David will be re-established and the nations of the world will come to join the people of God. 'Abandon your old ways in Babylon,' says the Lord, 'and seek the higher ways of my kingdom in the new Jerusalem.'

The above interpretation of this passage is based on its context in the section from Isaiah 54:11–55:13, and it draws out a comparison between the teaching of the prophet and the teaching of Jesus. Jesus was always inviting people to enter the kingdom of God, and, according to Mark, his opening message was, 'The time is ripe; the kingdom of God has drawn near. Change your way of thinking, and believe the good news.' Jesus described the kingdom in terms of a wedding feast (Matthew 22:1-14) and said that it was not like the kingdoms of the world because it was based on peace and not violence (John 18:36) and was an expression of God's justice (Matthew 6:33). He also said it was a kingdom open to all nations (Luke 13:29). In most of these things Isaiah and Jesus preached the same message.

But the kingdom described by Jesus was unlike the kingdom of David because it was more elusive. The idea of a kingdom today is a bit outdated and not part of most people's everyday experience. Now we go in for democratic republics or presidential dictatorships. But the decline in earthly kingdoms need not weaken the idea of the kingdom of God in people's minds; it may actually strengthen it because it then takes on a mythological aura associated with all the kingdoms we've read about in story. The kingdom of God can then be seen as a vision, an ideal or a dream, but it is unlike any human vision, dream or ideal because it is God's idea of what the world could be like, given the willing cooperation of the human race. And it is a vision not bounded by time or place because it exists in time in human minds and eternally in the mind of God, and it exists in any place where someone seeks to do God's will. That is why Jesus could say that the kingdom of God is both within us and among us (Luke 17:21).

The feast of the kingdom is the marriage feast of heaven and earth because the kingdom of heaven comes down to earth (as the new Jerusalem comes down from heaven – Revelation 21:2) when the values of heaven are transposed into our worldly situation – when love and justice replace hate and oppression, and when hope and peace triumph over despair and conflict. And God has invited us to that wedding feast.

When we are invited to a wedding we don't ask ourselves whether we deserve to go; we write back and accept the invitation with thanks. We may refuse because it clashes with something else but usually we will make arrangements to clear our diaries for that special date. And when we're invited to a wedding by God nothing should stop us from accepting the invitation, because what could be more important than being present at the marriage of heaven and earth? We will take our gifts, of course, and make sure we wear our best clothes (Colossians 3:12-14), but otherwise we only need to turn up to enjoy the feast and join in the celebration.

But let me abandon metaphors and write in plain words. You would think that if we ever got a chance to make the world a better place – by being kind in words and helpful in actions, by comforting someone in distress or forgiving someone who has hurt us, by being generous in sharing and honest in our dealings – you would think we would jump at the chance, because it is by such things as these that heaven comes down to earth. Yet, too often, we just make our excuses and turn the invitation down.

Day 22: Wednesday
Enjoying God

Psalm 95

Let us worship the Lord with songs of joy and gratitude because he is the Ruler of everything he has made. Let us bow down and worship him because he has made us and he is our shepherd. But God says, 'Then why don't you listen to me and obey me? You are as stubborn as your ancestors in the wilderness, who disobeyed me and failed to enter the Promised Land.'

Psalm 19:7-14

The Law of the Lord is perfect; his teaching is sound, his precepts are right and his commands are clear. They provide us with wisdom, happiness and understanding. So live in awe of God because he is just and his words are more precious than gold and sweeter than honey. They guide and reward those who heed them. Therefore take away my hidden faults and save me when I am tempted to deliberate sins, so that I may be blameless and innocent of great wrong. Accept the words of my meditation, Lord, for you are my strength and my redeemer.

Psalm 63:1-8

O my God, I thirst for you, like someone gasping for breath in a waterless desert. For I have seen your power and glory in the place of worship and I will praise you with upraised hands for your love and faithfulness all my life. When I meditate on you in the night my soul is richly fed and I praise you with joy. For you are my help and protector and I gladly hold fast to your right hand.

I once saw a film in which a mother and her children were waving goodbye to Dad who was staying at home. 'Enjoy yourselves!' he cried. 'Don't be silly, dear, we're going to church,' his wife replied.

I'd like to think the days were gone when people felt there was nothing enjoyable about religion – that it was all a matter of gloom, seriousness, guilt and fear. Modern music and less formal worship have played a large part in dispelling that image, although there are still many who get a great deal of enjoyment from traditional forms of worship and music. It's possible to go too far and turn worship into laugh-a-minute entertainment. In a Church of England promotion video a teenage girl asserted that 'Christianity is just about having fun, basically'. The time will surely come when she'll want more than just fun from religion.

All these psalmists had discovered something more than fun – they had discovered real delight in God. One experienced joy in worship, one found inspiration in the scriptures, and the other knew the wonder and the deep satisfaction of the experience of the presence of God, both in public worship and in private meditation. There is joy in religion because there is joy in God and the things of God. The Book of Job describes creation as the time when 'the morning stars sang together, and the sons of God shouted for joy' (Job 38:7), and Jesus tells us that 'there is joy in heaven' every time a sinner repents (Luke 15:7). He himself was able to face the cross because of 'the joy that lay ahead of him' (Hebrews 12:2).

We can't live at such high levels of emotion all the time because sorrow is an inevitable part of our earthly experience. There is a balance in these things. Sometimes our duties seem burdensome, but we can do them with delight because we do them for the Lord. At times worship seems dreary and mechanical, but 'sometimes a light surprises the Christian while he sings' (William Cowper). Sometimes the Bible seems obscure, but its words can fill us with new energy and insight. Even when we face real difficulties, joy can come and lift us above them all. When the Scottish minister, Samuel Rutherford, lay in jail, he wrote, 'Jesus Christ came to me in my cell last night, and every stone glowed like a ruby.'

So we need not think that God wants us to be miserable all the time, even in Lent, nor need we feel guilty because we aren't always full of joy. Nor should we think we are enjoying God when we are only enjoying ourselves and have forgotten how to listen and obey. Psalm 95 is a salutary reminder of this.

Day 23: Thursday
Grace, peace and hope

Romans 5:1-11

Because we believe that our sins have been cancelled by the forgiving love (grace) of God through Jesus Christ, we can be at peace with God and look forward to sharing in his glory. We can even rejoice in our troubles because they test our endurance and give us spiritual strength, so that we are filled with hope – a hope which does not let us down because the love of God has been poured into our hearts by the Holy Spirit. For God showed his love for us in that Christ died for us while we were still sinners. Since we have been put right with God by Christ's blood, how much more shall we be saved by him from God's just punishment? For if we have been reconciled to God by the death of his Son while we were his enemies, even more shall we be made whole by his life. We therefore rejoice in God through our Lord Jesus Christ, who has brought about our reconciliation.

Although I don't always understand St Paul's writings, I find that his words speak to me even when his sentences leave me bewildered. There are three particular words in this passage which stand out for me as I read it – grace, peace and hope.

Paul writes of grace here meaning the forgiving love of God, his mercy and free pardon. Grace is God's attitude and gift to us, not to be won but to be received by faith. It has been revealed to us in the fact that 'Christ died for us while we were still sinners'. It is on the rock of this grace that we 'stand', as Paul puts it. Certainly, without it we fall. When Paul was wrestling with his 'thorn in the flesh' he received a personal reassurance from God – 'My grace is sufficient for you' (2 Corinthians 12:9) – which has continued to reassure many others in similar circumstances.

In another place Paul wrote, 'By the grace of God I am what I am' (1 Corinthians 15:10), and though he was thinking specifically of his calling as an Apostle, his words can be extended to mean not only that we owe our redemption or our calling to God but that we owe our very existence to him. God is our redeemer *and* our creator. Only occasionally does it strike us how amazing and unfathomable our existence is, and that it is all by the grace of God!

When we realise that we 'stand' on the rock of God's grace, we discover a peace which the world cannot give (John 14:27), a peace that 'passes all understanding' (Philippians 4:7). And it is a peace which can stay with us even in our troubles because, no matter what our circumstances, we are always upheld by the grace of God. Sheila Walsh, who was a highly successful Gospel singer and TV chat-show presenter in the USA, had a nervous breakdown due to overwork. She checked in to a psychiatric hospital and was diagnosed as suffering from clinical depression. She discovered during her slow recovery that God was actually present with her in her suffering and that she was loved more than she'd ever imagined. 'I look on that time as one of God's greatest gifts to me,' she said. 'I never knew that God lived so close to the floor.' She discovered that, no matter how far down she had fallen, 'underneath were the everlasting arms' (Deuteronomy 33:27).

Paul's third word is hope. The Christian Gospel is a message of hope because it is grounded on faith in the grace of God, and this points us forward to the possibility of better things. If creation were a total accident, we could have no such confidence because nature speaks with a divided voice. We can delight in the present beauty of the world but we know that all things are subject to change and decay. We ourselves are subject to death and, apart from the gospel, do not know what, if anything, lies beyond death. But we believe that Christ not only died but rose again. His death assures us of God's good will towards us, and his resurrection confirms God's loving power and purposes. So, no matter what may happen to us in this 'vale of tears', we can always hope, and our hope is founded, like peace, on the rock of God's grace. It is a hope not of some perfect utopia created by politicians and bureaucrats but of God's own eternal kingdom in which we will share in the glory of God.

Day 24: Friday
You have been warned

Luke 13:1-9

When some people told Jesus about the Galileans whom Pilate killed while they were offering sacrifices, he warned them not to think that those Galileans were worse sinners than any other Galileans, but to repent of their own sins in case the same thing happened to them. Similarly, said Jesus, 'the people in Siloam who were killed when a tower fell on them were no worse sinners than anyone else, but you should all turn from your sins or you will die like them. Then he told the story of a man who had a fig tree in his vineyard but for three years it had produced no fruit. When he told the gardener to chop it down, the gardener said, 'Give it one more year, while I nurture it, and if it still bears no fruit, then I will chop it down.'

1 Corinthians 10:1-13

Paul reminds his readers how God rescued his people from Egypt by bringing them safely across the Red Sea and providing them with food and drink in the desert. But, even so, most of them died in that wilderness because they turned from God to worship idols and practise immorality. But Christians should not do the same, nor should they test the Lord, like the Israelites, nor grumble and complain like them, for they died from snake bites and disease. Their example warns us who think we stand safe on the Rock of Christ to take care lest we fall. We are all tested, like everybody else, but God never allows us to be tested beyond our limits. He always gives us the strength to survive the test.

It is a strange perversion of faith which takes it for granted that the road ahead will be smooth and safe because God is with us. It wasn't for Jesus, and we shouldn't expect it to be for us. Nevertheless it is easy to slip into this kind of complacency. Even in everyday life when we hear of deaths by road accidents, fires or heart attacks and so on, we don't usually think the same things will happen to us –

not today, anyway. However, if we have any sense we will take them as warnings – to drive more carefully, fit smoke alarms or take more care of our health. If we don't, we're asking for trouble.

Similarly, as Christians, we would be foolish to be complacent and believe that God will protect us, no matter what. In 1997, when Andy Green drove the supersonic car *Thrust* through the sound barrier at between 700 and 800 miles per hour, he didn't put his safety down to his faith in God but to the care and engineering expertise of his team. 'If I do something silly,' he said, 'God isn't going to suspend the laws of gravity to save Andy Green.'

But Jesus and Paul aren't just talking about 'doing something silly'; they are talking about doing something morally wrong. And that can have even more dangerous consequences than doing something silly because it means that we are turning away from God and taking his patience for granted. We cannot survive as individual Christians if we forget our dependence on God, and we cannot survive as churches if we are not responsive to God's prompting or obedient to his will. Nor can our society survive if it ignores God's commandments. Nor can the world survive if its people persist with a programme of self-destruction. Just as the prophets warned the people of their own day that idolatry, injustice and immorality would lead to national disaster, so Jesus warned his fellow Jews and Paul warned his fellow Christians that complacency would lead to 'death' (and there is more than one way of interpreting that word).

God is patient with our faults and failures, just as the gardener in Jesus' parable was patient with the fruitless fig tree. But there is a limit even to the patience of God, and the destruction of Jerusalem by the Babylonians and then the Romans bears witness to it. Can we take for granted God's patience with either the Church or the world if they fail to bear the fruit of righteousness which God is looking for?

Day 25: Saturday
The foolishness of God

1 Corinthians 1:18-25

The message of the cross is foolishness to those who are perishing, but to those who are being saved it is the power of God. It is written: 'I will destroy the wisdom of the wise and put aside the understanding of the intelligent' (Isaiah 29:14). Where are the wise and the scribe and the philosopher of this age? Has not God made foolish the wisdom of this world? For since, in God's wisdom, the world did not know God by wisdom, God was pleased to save those that believe by the foolishness of the Christian message. Jews ask for a sign and Greeks seek wisdom, but we preach Christ crucified, which is offensive to the Jews and foolishness to the Greeks, but to those who are called it is Christ – God's power and wisdom – because the foolishness of God is wiser than human wisdom, and the weakness of God is stronger than human strength.

The tension between the limited wisdom of human beings and the infinitely greater wisdom of God is apparent everywhere in the scriptures. 'For my thoughts are not like your thoughts, and your ways are not like my ways,' says the Lord, via his prophet (Isaiah 55:8). God works out his plans and purposes in surprising ways, and is always the God of the unexpected. Consider the story of Joseph, whose dreams were fulfilled in a totally unpredictable way; or the story of Moses, brought up in an Egyptian palace and wasting his days looking after his father-in-law's flocks, but then being called by God to lead his people from slavery in Egypt to freedom in the Promised Land. Who would have thought it? Not Moses, certainly. And who would have thought that God's holy city of Jerusalem and its holy Temple would be destroyed by foreigners and his people carried off into exile, only to return 70 years later and begin to rebuild their nation? Only the prophets, who had learned it from God. And who would have thought that the Messiah would come as the son of a carpenter, with no political or military power, and allow himself to be crucified by the Romans? Only Jesus himself, who believed he was fulfilling God's plan. And who would have thought that he would rise again from death on the third day? Certainly not his friends and followers, who were totally bewildered by the whole turn of events.

We often think God is miles behind us because he seems so slow to act, but in truth he is always at least one step ahead of us, though we only realise it when we look back and see how things have turned out. He works today with an eye not on tomorrow but on the day after tomorrow – the third day.

And just as God's actions are beyond our understanding, so are his thoughts. Matthew collected some of the moral teaching of Jesus into what we call the Sermon on the Mount, and that sermon has always challenged the thinking of the world in very radical ways, yet the world very often regards it as foolishness. Love your enemies? Don't resist evil? Don't store up treasure on earth? Don't worry about food, drink or clothing? Don't judge other people? The meek shall inherit the earth? You've got to be joking! And yet Jesus insisted that these teachings were the solid wisdom on which we must build our lives. Everything else is only the sand of foolishness. And the remarkable thing about Jesus is that he not only taught these things but he actually lived them, even though it brought him to death on a cross. The result is that on this solid wisdom, which many regard as foolishness, he founded a kingdom that will outlast all the kingdoms of this world. As Napoleon Bonaparte once said, 'Alexander, Caesar, Charlemagne and I have founded great empires; but upon what do these great creations depend? Upon force. Jesus has founded his empire upon love, and to this day millions would die for him.'

Such is the foolishness of God. But, as Paul said, 'The foolishness of God is wiser than human wisdom, and his weakness is stronger than human strength', though we are still reluctant to believe it.

Day 26: The Fourth Sunday in Lent
The blind see

John 9:1-41

Jesus heals a man on the Sabbath who has been blind from birth. The Pharisees interrogate the man but he refuses to be intimidated. They question his parents but they don't want to get involved. So they call the man back for more questioning but he stands his ground and sarcastically asks how it is that they, who are religious leaders, don't know how Jesus could have cured him. They expel him from the synagogue. Jesus finds the man again and asks him if he believes in the Son of Man. When the man who had been blind learns that Jesus is the Son of Man, he kneels down and says, 'I believe, Lord.' Jesus says, 'I have come to judge this world so that the blind shall see and those who see shall become blind'; at which some Pharisees say, 'Are we blind, then?' And Jesus replies, 'If you really thought you were blind you would have some excuse, but since you think you can see, you remain guilty.'

This is a marvellous story which needs to be read in full in order to try and catch all its nuances and enjoy all its humour. Like all John's Gospel it has both a surface meaning and a deeper meaning, which needs to be discovered by faith.

One of the main themes of John's Gospel is the coming of the light and the ability, or lack of ability, of human beings to see that light and to see by it. The coming of the light is announced in the very first chapter (1:4, 5, 9). But human beings couldn't recognise the one who brought the light (1:10, 11) because no human being had ever seen God before, but Jesus came to reveal God's true nature (1:18). Christ, the Light of the World, reveals the invisible reality of God to all who believe and enables them to walk out of darkness into light (8:12; 9:5).

That is why seeing is so important to John; it represents believing. The blind see when their eyes of faith are opened to the light of God in Jesus Christ. Jesus's first words to his future disciples in this Gospel were 'What are you looking for?' And his response to their answer was 'Come and see' (1:38, 39). And that is what this story about the blind man being given his sight by Jesus is all about.

We are all born blind – we don't see God, we don't know God – until Jesus comes and opens our eyes. The Pharisees in the story think they can see. They think they know what God is like and, to them, he is nothing like Jesus, and Jesus is nothing like God (9:16a, 24, 29). But when the man born blind has been given his sight he gradually begins to see that Jesus really is a man sent from God. First he says, 'He is a prophet' (9:17); then he says that because Jesus was able to open his eyes he can't be a sinner, because God only listens to those who worship him and do his will. Therefore this man must be 'from God' (9:30-33); and in the end he believes that Jesus is 'the Son of Man' and kneels down to pay homage to him (9:35-38).

Our human understanding of God is very limited and very distorted, and we always tend to make God in our own image, even when we should know better. So we end up creating a God who is as aggressive and vindictive and judgemental as *we* are, whereas Jesus has shown us that God is as merciful, as generous and as loving as *he* is. People believed in those days that God punished sinners by making them or their children blind from birth; Jesus showed us that God wants to help the blind to see.

Ironically, when Saul of Tarsus encountered the living Christ on the road to Damascus, he was temporarily blinded by the dazzling brightness, but when Ananias laid his hands on him, his sight was restored and he saw everything (Jesus, God, himself and the world around him) in a completely new light.

So Jesus came to bring the light of truth into the world – the truth about God, and therefore the ultimate truth about everything (John 18:37). This world is not a meaningless accident but part of God's creative plan to bring all things into union with himself and share in his glory (Ephesians 1:9, 10; John 17:20-24). This purpose is expressed in the first words attributed to God in the Bible: 'Let there be light' (Genesis 1:3) – the light of beauty, the light of goodness, and the light of consciousness.

Day 27: Monday
Don't judge by appearances

1 Samuel 16:1-13

The Lord tells Samuel not to be sorry that Saul has been rejected as king but to go to Jesse of Bethlehem and anoint one of his sons as the new king. After seeing all but one of Jesse's sons, Samuel is told by the Lord to anoint the youngest one – the shepherd boy, David.

Probably the best known words in this story are in verse 7, when the Lord tells Samuel not to take any notice of how tall or good-looking Jesse's sons are – 'because the Lord doesn't see as human beings see. They judge by outward appearances, but the Lord looks into the heart.' So Samuel quickly rejects seven of Jesse's sons, even though he had been tempted to choose the first one on the basis of his appearance. And when he sees David, he notes his fresh complexion, his bright eyes and his handsome features, but, having been told that the Lord doesn't judge by outward appearances, he probably wouldn't have chosen him either, if the Lord hadn't stepped in and told him to. So what did the Lord see in David's heart that Samuel didn't? We can only guess, but perhaps it was David's courage and his faith – both of which were soon to be tested by the challenge from Goliath.

Judging by outward appearances, rather than by qualities of character, is a common human failing. If we meet someone who is well-dressed and well-spoken, we are more likely to be impressed by them than by someone who is poorly dressed and roughly spoken, even in church, where *everybody* is supposed to be welcome (see James 2:2-4). Many women have married bad husbands and men have been attracted to unsuitable women because they judged them purely on appearances. Confidence tricksters can even make a living out of appearing to be what they are not, and most people try putting on appearances from time to time. But God sees into our hearts.

And Jesus had the gift of being able to see below the surface to what was inside people (John 2:25). He knew that Peter would deny him and Judas would betray him. He knew those who were like whitewashed tombs – outwardly beautiful but full of dead men's bones within (Matthew 23:27). And he could also see beyond Peter's weakness to his potential strength (John 1:42). Jesus knows us as we really are, not as we pretend to be, and only a friend who knows us as we really are can help us to cope with our weaknesses and discover what we can become. Jesus is such a friend.

One difficulty in all this is discerning the call of God. If God knows what we are like and also knows our true potential, and we feel called by him to a certain work, we should be confident that he is calling us to do something we are capable of, with his help. But this is not always the case. Sometimes people feel called but their call is rejected by the Church or some other body. Or they may feel called and their call is accepted, but then they go on to fail in their calling. If God knows what he's doing, presumably neither of these situations should arise.

The problem could be that we aren't being called by God at all but we only think we are; and that feeling is not based on God's judgement of us but on our false judgement of ourselves. Perhaps many would like to be brain surgeons but few are chosen. On the other hand, Gladys Aylward felt called to be a missionary in China – a view not shared by the China Inland Mission – yet her faith and determination enabled her to fulfil her calling in a remarkable way.

Some biblical stories about people who are called by God illustrate a different point. They show that those called often doubt their own potential and have to be strongly persuaded by God to go ahead – Moses and Jeremiah, for example. Maybe there are some who manage to resist the call of God all their lives, and there are certainly many who put it off for years before finally responding, and wishing they'd done it earlier.

The truth behind all this seems to be that God does call people into his service, and he does know what he is doing. It is we who sometimes get it all wrong.

Day 28: Tuesday
Food in the desert, and beyond

Psalm 23

The Lord, my shepherd, leads me to places of refreshment, along right paths and through the valley of shadows. He offers me rich hospitality, and his goodness and mercy are with me all my days. I shall dwell in his house for ever.

Psalm 107:1-9

Thank the Lord for his goodness and unfailing love, all you he has set free and brought back home from exile. Those of you who were lost in the desert cried to the Lord for help and he gave you food and drink and led you safely to a city.

Joshua 5:9-12

After all the men of Israel had been circumcised at Gilgal, the Lord said to Joshua, 'Today I have lifted from you the curse of Egypt'; then they celebrated Passover on the Plains of Jericho. And the day after that they ate food grown in the Land of Canaan for the first time, unleavened bread and roasted grain; and the supplies of manna came to an end.

One thing I have learned over and over again in life (and which I've quickly forgotten every time) is that God's supplies do not dry up in the desert. They are constantly renewed, like manna from heaven and water from the rock. At low points in my journey, just when I was thinking of giving up, abandoning faith and losing hope, I have been revived again, often in unexpected ways. I'm sure many others have found the same. And that's why I've always been moved by Longfellow's well-known words about the inner refreshment we sometimes receive from unknown sources 'far off'.

As torrents in summer, half dried in their channels,
suddenly rise, though the sky is still cloudless,
for rain has been falling far off at their fountains;
so hearts that are fainting grow full to o'erflowing,
and they that behold it, marvel and know not
that God at their fountains far off has been raining.

Take the example of Handel – we know he was given the inspiration to write *Messiah* in the space of three weeks when a stroke left him paralysed and his creditors were clamouring to be paid. It is as if adversity squeezes music out of some people's souls, just as a kettle sings loudest when it's up to its neck in hot water.

We also know that the Desert Fathers deliberately went into the wilderness to seek God in prayer because they knew there was food in the desert which could refresh their spirits.

This doesn't mean that the desert is the only place where God feeds us. Psalm 23 reminds us that the Lord has prepared a table for us where our cups will overflow with wine. We have a foretaste of this in the sacrament of Holy Communion, but the banquet of the kingdom prepared for all humankind will be even finer. The passage from Psalm 107 paints a similar picture. Those who have wandered in the deserts of exile have been led back to the homeland in Jerusalem where God will satisfy the thirsty and fill the hungry with good things. The passage from Joshua tells how the people finally arrive in Canaan, the Land of Promise and of milk and honey. The desert manna is no longer required. So there is a richer satisfaction waiting for us in the kingdom of God than anything in the wilderness of the present world.

These images of eternal hope are described in very material terms, but they represent spiritual realities beyond our understanding, which at present we can only experience from afar. If and when we do experience them fully we shall no doubt feel like the church caretaker who was given an expensive present on his retirement and said, 'Goodness and mercy have followed me all the days of my life, but this is the first time they've ever caught up with me.'

Day 29: Wednesday
Rise and shine

Ephesians 5:8-14

Once you were in darkness, but now that you are in the light of the Lord, live like children of light, bearing the fruit of light, which is found in everything good, right and true. Learn what is pleasing to the Lord, and have nothing to do with the works of darkness, except to expose them to the light, so that they can be seen for the shameful and unspeakable things they are. That is why we say, 'Awake, sleeper, and rise from the dead; and Christ will give you light.'

Ephesians 2:1-10

He brought you to life when you were dead in your sins; for that is how you once behaved when you walked in the way of the world, following the worldly spirit of disobedience. That is how we all lived, ruled by the passions of the flesh and the lusts of both body and mind, being subject to God's wrath, like everybody else. But God, in his rich mercy and his great love for us, brought us to life with Christ, while we were still dead in our sins (for it is by grace that you are saved). And he raised us up together and seated us in the heavenly places with Christ Jesus, that he might show to future times the unlimited wealth of his grace in his kindness towards us through Christ Jesus. For you are saved by grace through faith, and you have not won this for yourselves – it is God's gift – you haven't earned it by anything you've done, so that you might boast about it. For it is God who has made us, created in Christ Jesus for the good works which God has prepared for us to do.

One of the spiritual moments for me when I get up in the morning is drawing back the curtains and letting the light flood into the house. Night's darkness has passed and a new day has begun. That image of moving from darkness into light is common in the New Testament because it was the very real experience of the early

Christians, especially Gentile Christians. They had been raised by Christ from the darkness of paganism and the immorality of Roman society at its worst, into the light of the family of God (1 Peter 2:9). In his letters to Corinth in particular, Paul leaves us in no doubt about the murky background from which many of his converts had come (for example, 1 Corinthians 6:9-11).

But, whatever our background, we are all called as Christians to rise and shine: 'Awake, sleeper . . . and Christ will give you light.' One of the startling things Jesus said to his disciples, and to the listening crowd, was 'You are the light of the world . . . Let your light shine' (Matthew 5:14a, 16a). Those words are also addressed to all of us because, as it is written in the Book of Proverbs, 'The human spirit is the candle of the Lord' (Proverbs 20:27, *Authorised Version*). Every human being has the potential to shine with the light of God; the candle only needs to be lit by the Spirit of God.

The world desperately needs that light to shine – the light of goodness, generosity, kindness, honesty and hope in human beings everywhere. As the Chinese say, 'It is better to light a candle than to curse the darkness' – so let your light shine. The nineteenth-century American preacher, Phillips Brooks, said that 'No man or woman can be strong, gentle, pure and good, without the world being better for it, without someone being helped and comforted by the very existence of that goodness.' Certainly, when we meet people who shine with a genuine goodness our own spirits are lit up by it. So, 'Let *your* light shine,' says Jesus.

This should not be a self-conscious process, but simply the effect of living close to Jesus and walking in his light. When Robert Louis Stevenson was a boy in Edinburgh, he was looking out of the window one evening watching the lamplighter go down the street lighting up the gas lamps with his long pole, and he turned to his mother and said, 'There's a man outside making holes in the darkness.' What a wonderful thing to do – making holes in the darkness. But the point is that the lamplighter probably wouldn't have thought of it like that. He was simply doing his job. So let's just follow Jesus, and leave it to him to give us light.

Day 30: Thursday
God's image

Numbers 21:4-9

The people complain to Moses about their hunger in the desert and the poor food they have to eat. Then fiery serpents come and bite them, so that many die. The people regard this as a punishment from the Lord for their grumbling, so they ask Moses to pray to the Lord to take the serpents away. The Lord tells Moses to make a bronze image of a fiery serpent and put it on a pole so that everyone who sees it will live.

John 3:14-21

Jesus says that just as Moses lifted up the serpent in the desert, so the Son of Man must be lifted up, that everyone who believes in him will have eternal life. God loved the world so much that he gave his Son to bring eternal life to all who believe. God didn't send the Son to condemn the world but to save it. Those who don't believe are judged because, having seen the light, they still prefer the darkness. Those who do what is true come to the light and live by it.

The strange story from the book of Numbers contains two things in particular which we no longer need to believe because Jesus Christ has shown us a better way. First of all we do not have to believe that God sends fiery serpents to punish us for our sins. This is a false idea of God. He is not vindictive, judgemental and bad-tempered – a grumpy old man in the sky, who seizes every opportunity to jump on us if we put a foot wrong – though many have believed this. I must admit that when I read the Book of Ezekiel through in one sitting as a young man, I definitely got this negative image of God in my mind. But I was wrong. When Jesus was asked why a certain man had been born blind, his questioners assumed that his blindness must have been God's punishment either for his or his parents' sins (John 9:1-3). But Jesus dismissed that idea and said that the man's blindness was not a punishment from God but rather an opportunity to do God's will by restoring the man's sight.

God is not hate, but love. He didn't send his Son into the world to condemn the world but to save it because he loved it so much. God's will is not for our destruction but for our good. Primitive instincts deep within us sometimes make us believe otherwise, but Jesus has shown us the truth about God by giving his life for our sakes, not by taking our lives to satisfy the demands of strict justice. Jesus has clearly revealed that mercy and grace are God's essential nature.

The other feature of the Old Testament story which Jesus has raised to a higher level is the setting up of a bronze serpent on a pole so that people could look on it and be saved from the fiery serpents. This action by Moses seems to contradict the second commandment, which prohibits the making of carved images to worship as gods. The bronze serpent, however, was not exactly worshipped but became a medium of healing for the people. Yet it could be that the story explains why some people may have established a cult of the bronze serpent in that particular place and worshipped it as God. But a bronze serpent is clearly an inadequate image of God, as are all our manufactured images, whether metal or mental. The only true image of God that we have is the one which he himself has given us – his own Son (see John 1:18 and Colossians 1:15). And as Moses lifted up the bronze serpent on a pole in the desert, so the Son of Man was lifted up on a cross outside a city wall. The crucifixion of Jesus gives us an image of God which supersedes all other images of him because it shows that his true nature is not vindictive judgement but sacrificial love.

Day 31: Friday
The ministry of reconciliation

2 Corinthians 5:16–6:10

We no longer judge other people by human standards, but we see every-one, including Christ himself, with new eyes because Christ has brought about a new order of things by reconciling us all to God. He has also called us to exercise a ministry of reconciliation, by preaching the mes-sage of reconciliation to the whole world as Christ's ambassadors. There-fore we try not to put anyone off by our ministry, but commend ourselves to you as God's servants, by enduring hardships, by showing genuine love and integrity, and by relying on the power of God in all circumstances.

There is nothing worse than Christians who have received the mes-sage of reconciliation but who exercise a ministry of confrontation. They are happy to regard *themselves* as God's friends but not so keen to regard others in the same light.

I recently got into conversation with the lady in charge of our local refuse tip, and I can't remember how the topic arose, but she said that her father stopped going to church because he was put off by all the back-biting and malicious gossip which went on there. I tried to point out that there are a large number of genuinely good people in the churches, but I don't think she was persuaded. That brief conversation certainly made me think very seriously about my own attitude and behaviour in this respect.

Perhaps the greatest tragedy in Christian history is the way in which Christians have regarded each other not as friends but as enemies if they didn't happen to belong to their own 'true' Church. It is said that John Wesley once dreamt that he went to hell, and as he was shown around he asked if there were any Methodists there. 'Oh yes,' was the reply, 'there are lots of them.' Wesley then asked if there were any Catholics, Presbyterians or Baptists there, and he got the same answer. He was then taken up to heaven, where he asked the question again – were there any Methodists, Catholics, Presbyterians or Baptists in heaven? This time the answer was, 'No there aren't any of them in heaven. There are only Christians.'

It is just as bad when Christians regard other cultural, national, racial and religious groups with suspicion or hostility. People are inevitably different from one another, not only because of their background history but also because of their individuality. If only we would value our differences instead of looking on them as an opportunity for confrontation. We have seen many examples in the modern world where people in conflict have realised that the only way forward is by means of negotiation, not trying to bomb the other side into submission.

The ministry of reconciliation is by no means easy, and those who exercise it have to be prepared for a rough ride as they try to overcome fear, distrust, bitterness and many setbacks along the way. But by patience, determination, honesty and courage, they can often turn breakdowns into breakthroughs and achieve agreements which nobody would have thought possible before negotiations began. Diplomacy is required in such situations, and diplomacy is a skill which all ambassadors need, including ambassadors for Christ.

Unfortunately, Christian evangelism has not always been diplomatic. It has too often been aggressive, Bible-bashing emotional blackmail and has described itself in military terms, such as crusade, campaign or mission. But there is a gentler (and more lasting) form of evangelism, which Jesus described in terms of sowing seeds. A sower went out to sow and, in spite of many setbacks, he stuck to his task and was rewarded in the end with a fruitful harvest. The message of God's love for the world is not one to be shouted into unreceptive ears but to be declared by means of loving attitudes and a real understanding of other people's forms of belief.

That is why, in a world where many religions meet, we need to take Wesley's dream a stage further and say that God has room in heaven for more than just Christians; he has room for all those whom he loves – and who are we to decide who *they* are?

Day 32: Saturday
Welcome home

Luke 15:1-3, 11b-32

Some scribes and Pharisees criticised Jesus for mixing with the outcasts of society. So Jesus told them a story about a younger brother who asked his father for his share of the family property and then went off to a distant country and wasted every penny in extravagant living. When a famine came he had to get a job as pig keeper, and in his desperate hunger he began to realise how much better off he would have been at home. So he decided to go back and ask his father to take him on as a hired servant because he didn't deserve to be called his son any more. As he got near home, his father saw him and rushed out to welcome him with a warm embrace. Before the boy had the chance to ask his father to give him a job on the farm, his father had ordered the servants to dress his son in the finest clothes and prepare a banquet to celebrate his return. But when the elder brother heard the sound of music and dancing as he came in from the fields, and found out what had happened, he was furious and refused to join the party. Forgetting that he too had received his share of his father's property, he complained that his father had never done anything like this for him but only for his wastrel brother. But the father gently reminded his elder son of all his blessings and told him that the return of his lost brother was something well worth celebrating.

This is one of those stories which appeals to every generation, and it will never lose its appeal until we all finally arrive in our eternal home, after much wandering. It can, like most other parables, be interpreted in many ways. In its context in Luke's Gospel it seems to refer to those Jews who lived outside the law and were not regarded as respectable by the religious authorities. Yet it was among such social outcasts that Jesus was often to be found – as if to say that the Father's love was for them also.

Perhaps the early Church saw the story as referring to the welcome given to the Gentiles when they responded to the preaching of the Gospel, even though certain Jewish Christians wanted to insist that Gentile converts be circumcised before becoming members of the Church.

Nowadays we might interpret it in terms of a worldwide secularism in which many people are turning away from God and religion, and making up their own minds about how they should live in the world and use up its resources. In this interpretation the earth which humankind have inherited is being recklessly laid waste by the demands of our extravagant lifestyles, which are increasingly threatened by a variety of disasters (represented by the famine in the parable). But God our Father is waiting patiently for us to come to our senses and return to the ways that he has taught us.

An individual interpretation of the story seems to be the most popular. After all, most people leave home at some time in their lives and go out into the world in search of happiness or fulfilment. Many leave God behind in the process and then perhaps return to faith in later life, to find that God has loved them all the while and is glad to have them home. Whether our lives have been successes or failures (humanly speaking) in our journey through the world, we become aware of our personal weaknesses and imperfections over the years, and our sins and sufferings leave their mark on us. It is then that we might seek forgiveness, acceptance and healing, and eventually find them in God.

On the other hand, there is something of the elder brother in us too. We feel resentment because some seem to do very well in life, in spite of (or even because of) their obvious sins and failings, while we who have plodded on our humdrum way, trying to be respectable citizens, receive precious few of the world's rewards and not a lot (it seems) of God's blessings. This sour-grapes attitude of bitterness and jealousy is quite common in us, and sometimes we have to be very forceful if we want to prevent it from appearing in public. But Jesus' parable happily and gently reminds us that God loves us too, and that we also are invited to his welcome-home party.

Day 33: The Fifth Sunday in Lent
Facing death

John 11:1-45

Martha and Mary sent a message to Jesus from their home in Bethany to tell him that their brother Lazarus was ill. Jesus was on the other side of the Jordan but he waited for two days before setting off for Bethany with his disciples. He was going to wake Lazarus from his sleep, he said. When Jesus approached Bethany, Martha came to meet him and tell him that Lazarus had died, and she wished Jesus had arrived earlier, but even now he could do something. Jesus said, 'Your brother will rise again.' Martha replied, 'I know that he will rise again in the final resurrection.' Jesus said, 'I am the resurrection and the life. Whoever believes in me shall live, even though they die; and whoever lives and believes in me shall never die.' Martha went back to the house and told Mary that Jesus wanted to see her. Mary went out quickly to meet him and the mourners followed her. Mary fell at Jesus' feet and said, 'If only you had been here earlier, Lord.' When Jesus saw her weeping and heard the mourners wailing, he was overcome with emotion and asked where Lazarus had been laid. They said, 'Come and see.' And Jesus wept. Still deeply moved, Jesus came to the tomb and asked for the stone to be rolled away. Martha objected that there would be a strong smell, but Jesus said, 'If you believe, you will see the glory of God.' Jesus prayed, and then shouted, 'Lazarus, come out!' The dead man came out wrapped in grave clothes. Jesus said, 'Unwrap him and let him go.' And many of the mourners who saw it believed in Jesus.

All of us have to face the fact of death and try to make some sense of it. In this story John tells of many people who are looking death in the face in different ways. Lazarus was facing imminent death because of his illness; Mary and Martha were grieving because of the death of their brother; Jesus was facing death in two senses – the death of his friend (and the grief of Martha and Mary) and his own death which he knew was not far away. The disciples were also conscious of the threats that had been made to Jesus' life and didn't want him to go back to Judea into real danger. They also feared that they would share that danger and perhaps die with him.

Death was in the thoughts of everyone involved in this story, and they all had to come to terms with it. Throughout most of the Old Testament death was regarded as the end – like dust returning to dust (Genesis 3:19); 'like water spilt on the ground, which cannot be gathered up again' (2 Samuel 14:14); like withered flowers and fleeing shadows (Job 14:2). 'There is hope for a tree that has been cut down because it may sprout again . . . but when human beings die . . . They lie down and do not rise again' (Job 14:7a, 10, 12a).

This Old Testament view of death is quite common today in our secular society. Sir Robert Winston ended his television series on the human body with a look at death. He said, 'We lose our selves when we die . . . *We* die; only our genes are immortal.' Many people think like that from time to time; and it is possible to find comfort in such a view because then death becomes like an endless sleep, which brings eternal peace – except that we aren't conscious of it.

This negative idea of death as the end means that our cups and saucers will last longer than we do, and in a thousand years' time someone will display them in museums to show how we lived. This suggests that the only significance of each individual is their contribution to the race. Once that contribution has been made, they can be dispensed with. But try telling that to those who mourn.

Jesus spoke about death as a sleep on several occasions, but for him it was a sleep from which it was possible to awake. He had a positive view of death which regarded it as an opportunity to reveal the glory of God, and he only went to funerals in order to raise the dead to life. We find it difficult to understand these things because our experience of death fills us with negative feelings, and we can't know what actually happens at the point of death until it happens to us. But at least we can believe. Martha believed, and we usually think of her as the practical and down-to-earth one. Perhaps she was nearer to heaven than we have imagined.

Day 34: Monday
God's promises

Ezekiel 37:1-14

The Spirit of the Lord brought Ezekiel to a valley absolutely full of very dry bones, and said to him, 'Son of man, can these bones live?' 'Only God knows that,' said Ezekiel. So the Spirit said, 'Tell these bones to hear the word of the Lord.' When Ezekiel obeyed, the bones began to come together with a great rattling noise, and flesh began to cover them. Then the Spirit commanded Ezekiel to call on the four winds to fill the dead bodies with breath. And when he did so, the bodies stood up on their feet like a mighty army. Then the Spirit explained that the bones were like the people of Israel, whose hope was dried up in the desert of exile. He told Ezekiel to go and preach to them that God would raise them from the grave and bring them back home to Israel. Then they would know that he was the Lord, and he would fill them with his Spirit.

Jeremiah 31:31-34

'The day will come,' says the Lord, 'when I will make a new covenant with Israel and Judah. It won't be like the covenant I made with them on Sinai – the covenant which they broke. No, it will be like this: I will put my Law in their heart, and I will be their God, and they will be my people. No one will need to tell their neighbour to know the Lord because they will all know me, from the humblest to the greatest; for I will forgive their perversity and forget their sin for ever.'

One of the remarkable things about the prophets was that they were so confident that God would fulfil his purposes, even though present circumstances made most people doubt that. Ezekiel was carried off from Jerusalem to Babylon with the first batch of exiles at the beginning of the sixth century BC. Like Jeremiah, he warned the people of the imminent destruction of Jerusalem. Nobody believed him, or Jeremiah, but the destruction of the Holy City duly took place at the hands of the Babylonians in 586 BC. Many more exiles arrived in Babylon, and Ezekiel set about encouraging them to believe that God would bring his people back to Jerusalem. His vision of the valley of dry bones is a telling picture of the low estate in which the exiles found themselves – and yet Ezekiel prophesied that God had plans to restore them. They would rise from their Babylonian grave-yard like resurrected corpses and march back home.

How could Ezekiel believe that? Jerusalem had been ruthlessly destroyed by the armies of the greatest empire in the world at that time. But Ezekiel knew that God was greater than any empire, and his vision showed him that God planned to lead his people back to their own land. And sure enough, about 50 years later, the exiles did begin to return. Eventually they rebuilt Jerusalem and the Temple – all of which must have seemed highly unlikely in the time of Ezekiel. But God keeps his promises.

Jeremiah was given an even more unlikely prophecy – that even though their nation was about to be destroyed, God would make a new covenant with his people, writing the Law on their hearts instead of on stone. They had not obeyed God's Law and had often worshipped other gods, but the God of Israel was not going to abandon them altogether. He would forgive their sins and enable them to know him better than they had before. This promise did not begin to be fulfilled until the coming of Jesus Christ 600 years later. On the eve of his death, he gave his disciples bread to eat and wine to drink; and as he gave them the wine he said, 'This cup is the new covenant in my blood' (1 Corinthians 11:25). From that time God began to gather together a people of his own from all over the world, a people drawn by the sacrifice of Christ on Calvary, whose blood had sealed God's new covenant more firmly than the old covenant had been sealed by the blood of animals on Sinai. God keeps his promises, even though he takes his time.

In Matthew's account of the Last Supper Jesus said to his disciples, 'I tell you that from now on I shan't drink of the fruit of the vine until that day when I drink new wine with you in my Father's kingdom' (Matthew 26:29). And that's another promise!

Day 35: Tuesday
Mixed emotions

Psalm 130

I cry out to you from the depths, O Lord! Lord, hear my voice and listen to my cry! If you reckoned up our sins, who would not be found guilty? But you are a forgiving God and we worship you. My very soul waits for the Lord and his word fills me with hope. I wait for the Lord more keenly than watchmen wait for the morning, looking out for the first light of dawn. O Israel, keep on hoping in the Lord, for his love never fails and he is always able to save. He will set Israel free from all her sins.

Psalm 126

When the Lord brought us back to Jerusalem, it was like being in a dream. We laughed and shouted for joy. It was said among the nations, 'What great things the Lord has done for them!' Yes, the Lord has done great things for us and we are glad. Revive our fortunes, Lord, as the rain revives streams in the desert. Let those who sow their seed in tears gather the harvest with joy. Those who weep as they go out to sow will come back home with shouts of joy, bringing their sheaves with them.

There is the cry of the exiles in these Psalms – longing for God to help them in Psalm 130 and rejoicing in their return to Jerusalem in Psalm 126. They cried out 'from the depths' in exile, and, as they hoped, God heard their cry, just as he had heard their ancestors' cry in Egypt (Exodus 3:7), and he came to their aid.

So there is a whole range of strongly felt emotions here. On the one hand there is a cry for help from the depths of despair, a sense of guilt and a longing for forgiveness, hope mingled with the frustration of long waiting. And on the other hand there is the laughter, joy and gladness they felt on returning to Jerusalem, together with tears and weeping as they struggle to cultivate the wasted land, until the harvest turns their tears to shouts of joy – a roller-coaster of emotions, as people say nowadays. And we've all been there at some time or other – both in the depths and on the heights.

Feelings are an essential part of human nature. Someone who has no feelings at all isn't really alive. It's true that we would rather miss out on the painful feelings and only experience the pleasant and uplifting ones. But the fact is that they both go together. Love and suffering go together because we suffer for those we love when they are in trouble or when we are separated. But we wouldn't want to be without love in our lives, in spite of the pain it sometimes brings us. Hope and disappointment go together because if we never hoped for anything we would never be disappointed. But a life without hope would seem unbearably dull and pointless.

Our feelings, like those of the exiles, are usually determined by our circumstances. We feel low when things are going badly and high when they are going well. But the feelings of those who suffer from manic depression swing from low to high and back again regardless of circumstances. Their illness is due to a chemical imbalance in the brain which needs medical treatment. Such treatment can also help those who suffer from depression. In these cases chemical imbalance may occur because the body has become run-down through overwork or excessive stress or physical illness, and these things can happen to anybody. Hormone changes at various stages of life sometimes have the same effect, though not inevitably.

This close link between feelings and chemicals raises problems for religious people because we sometimes get the idea that if you believe in God you should feel happy all day long. But most people don't, and if they are religious they can feel guilty because they don't. Severe depression carries with it feelings of helplessness, hopelessness and worthlessness, which seem to contradict the expected nature of Christian life; and insensitive believers can even suggest that depression is due to the patient's lack of faith, when really it is due to lack of serotonin. This only goes to show that the presence of God does not depend on our ever-changing feelings but on the reality of his never-changing love.

Day 36: Wednesday
Perfect obedience

Psalm 119:9-16

How can a young man live a pure life? Only by living it in obedience to your word. I seek you with all my heart. May I not stray from your commandments? I have stored your word in my heart, so that I might not sin against you. O God, teach me your laws. I recite all your words and find pleasure in your teachings as much as in great riches. I will meditate on your instructions and concentrate on your ways. I will delight in your laws and never forget them.

Hebrews 5:5-10

Christ did not appoint himself as a high priest but was appointed by God, who said, 'You are my Son, whom I have begotten today,' and again, 'You are a priest for ever, in the order of Melchizedek.' In his earthly life, Jesus prayed to God with loud cries and tears to be saved from death; and he was heard because of his devotion to God. Though he was a Son, he learned to obey through suffering, and, having been made perfect, he became the author of eternal salvation to all those who obey him.

Everyone who believes that God is the highest good would want to echo the words of the Psalmist. He was a young man with great aims in life – nothing less than perfect obedience to the will of God as written in the Law. The Pharisees held this up as the great ideal, but they made it more difficult for themselves by expanding the Law to meet every possible situation, and were so concerned about the details that they missed the 'weightier matters' such as justice, mercy and faith (Matthew 23:23, 24).

The idea of perfection has always been a subject of debate in the Church. Jesus himself taught his followers that they must be perfect as their heavenly Father is perfect (Matthew 5:48). In the eighteenth century, John Wesley preached the possibility of attaining perfect love in this life. However, he never claimed that he himself had attained it. The problem is that we don't really know what perfection is, and since we live in a world of time, we can't be sure that once perfection is achieved it is going to last.

Nevertheless, most Christians are happy to say that Jesus was perfectly obedient to his Father's will, and that is why he is able to be a high priest on our behalf. All other high priests in the line of Aaron were sinful human beings, just like us, and though they could sympathise with sinful people they could not offer God perfect obedience on their behalf – only Jesus could do that. So we imperfect sinners are accepted by God in the name of the perfect human being, Jesus Christ. We are able to bask in his glory and benefit from his perfection, and we are allowed into heaven simply because we are Jesus' friends and not on merit. But if you think that lets you off being obedient, remember that Jesus said, 'You are my friends if you do what I command you' (John 15:14).

One of the great developments of the last few centuries is that dedicated men and women have learned how to obey the laws of the physical world – of physics and chemistry, for instance. And by their careful study of those laws they have achieved great things which our ancestors would have regarded as miracles.

But now we need to turn our attention to the laws of life – laws of morality, human relationships, social justice and 'shalom'. We have neglected this essential aspect of God's law for too long, to the point where the very existence of life on this planet is increasingly under threat. Our attitude to moral law is like the notice on the office wall: 'If all else fails, try doing what the boss said.' Can we afford to wait until all else fails before we start to obey the golden rule: 'Treat other people as you would have them treat you'?

We have known these moral truths for centuries, but, like Adam and Eve, we would rather ignore them and please ourselves. It is ironic that we are happy to be friends of the man who obeyed God's moral law perfectly but are reluctant to do so ourselves. The young Psalmist may have been too optimistic and idealistic but at least he was willing to give obedience a chance. Are we?

Day 37: Thursday
The fragrance of love

John 12:1-8

A week before Passover Jesus came to Bethany, where Martha served up a meal for him, and Lazarus was among the guests. Then Mary took a pound of expensive ointment and anointed Jesus's feet, wiping them with her hair, so that the house was filled with the fragrant smell of the ointment. But Judas Iscariot said, 'Why wasn't this ointment sold and the money given to the poor?' But he said this not because he cared for the poor but because he had the money bag and took whatever was put into it. So Jesus said, 'Leave her alone. She can keep the ointment for the day of my burial. You have the poor with you always; but you will not always have me.'

This story reminds us of a similar incident involving Martha and Mary in Luke 10:38-42. In both accounts Jesus is their guest and Martha serves up a meal while Mary sits at Jesus' feet. But on this occasion Martha is not harassed or critical of her sister, but both of them wait on Jesus in ways that suit their temperament: Martha with practical serving and Mary with warm, sensual affection. How many women have waited on Jesus in similar ways over the centuries, and still do today?

For though Christ is no longer with us in the flesh, he is with us in the bodies of our fellow human beings, especially those in desperate need of loving kindness. Everybody knows of the service of Mother Teresa and her sisters to the poor and dying. It was inspired by the words of Jesus in the parable of the sheep and the goats (Matthew 25:31-46), especially the words, 'Insofar as you did this [service] to the least of these brethren of mine, you did it to me.' Mother Teresa herself said, 'I see Christ in every person I touch . . . Every time I give a piece of bread, I give it to him.'

In spite of Judas' apparent concern for the poor (verse 5), we don't think he was really eager to serve them with his own hands. We are reminded of the words of St Paul: 'If I spend all I have in feeding the poor, but have no love, I gain nothing.' Love is shown in this story in the practical service of Martha and the soothing touch of Mary.

There has always been emphasis on the senses in Christian worship – the sound of speech and music, the sight of pictures, windows, carvings, robes, the smell of incense and flowers, the taste of bread and wine and the touch of hands. The Puritan tradition tempered such sensuality to some extent, but the modern Church in Britain is more open to the touchy-feely element in worship, though not everybody is happy with hugs and kisses during the service. (Ironically, even Judas was willing to greet Jesus with a kiss in the Garden of Gethsemane.)

Mary showed her love for Jesus with sensuous actions – rubbing his feet with ointment and wiping them with her hair – echoing some of the language of the Song of Songs (for example, 1:3,12; 4:10). No wonder the cold-hearted Judas objected.

Jesus was quick to defend Mary, as he was in Luke's story (10:41, 42), though his rebuke of Judas is mild, compared with the harsh words of the gospel writer. In the versions of Matthew and Mark, Jesus is even more fulsome in his appreciation of his anointing (see Matthew 26:10, 13; Mark 14:6, 9). I wonder if it was this incident which inspired Jesus to wash his disciple's feet at the last supper?

John tells us that the fragrant smell of the perfume filled the whole house, and some have interpreted this to refer to the way in which the love of Christians for their Lord and for one another can create a special 'atmosphere' within the life of the Church. St Paul speaks of the gifts he received from the Philippians as 'a fragrant offering, a sacrifice acceptable and pleasing to God' (Philippians 4:18); and in Ephesians 5:2 Christians are urged to 'walk in love, just as Christ loved us and gave himself up for us, a fragrant offering and sacrifice to God'. But Paul uses the image of fragrance again in 2 Corinthians 2:14-16, when he describes how the preaching of the gospel spreads the fragrance of the knowledge of Jesus beyond the Church, into the wider world. Maybe the kingdom of God will not only be full of glorious light but of sweet aromas too.

Day 38: Friday
Down or up?

Philippians 3:4b-14

I no longer rely on my racial and religious credentials for salvation, though I would be more qualified to do so than most people. I was born a Jew of the tribe of Benjamin; I was circumcised; as a Pharisee I was a meticulous observer of the Jewish Law; and I was a religious zealot to the point of persecuting the Church. But these things which I regarded as being of merit I now regard as total loss, compared with the knowledge of Jesus Christ my Lord, which is far superior to them. In order that I might gain Christ I have thrown out everything else as so much rubbish. It may seem that I have lost everything, but being found by Christ more than compensates for that. Therefore I no longer rely on obedience to the Law, but I put my faith in Christ in order to attain the righteousness of God. It's true that at present I share in Christ's death by suffering with him, but I shall also share in the power of his resurrection by being raised from the dead. Not that I have already received this or have already been made perfect, but I am pressing on to lay hold of that for which Christ lay hold of for me. Therefore, one thing I do: forgetting what lies behind and stretching out to what lies ahead, I press on towards the finishing line for the prize of God's upward call to life in Christ Jesus.

Romans 8:6-11

Concern for the demands of our lower nature brings death, but concern for the Spirit brings life and peace; because the fleshly mind is hostile to God, for it is not subject to the Law of God, nor can it be, and those whose lives are dominated by the demands of their lower nature cannot please God. But your main concern is not with your lower nature but with the Spirit, if in fact the Spirit of Christ dwells in you. (For whoever does not have the Spirit of Christ does not belong to him.) But if Christ is in you, the body is indeed dead because of sin, but the spirit is alive because of God's righteous mercy. But if the Spirit of him who raised up

Jesus from the dead dwells in you, by that same Spirit God will also give life to your mortal bodies.

Many forces are at work in our lives, pulling us in one direction or another, but two of the most obvious are the forces which pull us down and the forces which pull us up. In some moods and situations we feel that the downward forces are in control. Our sun is cooling down, our bodies are running down, and in autumn the leaves fall down; and there are moral influences which encourage us to look down and adjust our standards of behaviour in accordance with the lowest common denominator. All these appear to be natural processes which we are powerless to reverse. Left to themselves, things seem to find it easier to run down than to rise up. Decay and death are the inevitable end for everything. As some people delight to point out, we start dying from the moment we are born.

But, fortunately, that is not the whole truth. From the moment they are born, babies start to grow up, and though physical growth stops at various points, spiritual, emotional, intellectual and moral growth can continue as if to say that 'growing up' is what the whole of life is about. As trees raise their branches to the sky and flowers turn their faces to the sun, so human beings can grow towards higher ideals and a greater consciousness of God above.

Paul talks about the upward call of God in Christ Jesus because the kind of life we see in Jesus Christ is the highest and best that we know. God's upward call is present in the whole of life – in the creation of an expanding universe from nothing, in the process of evolution, in the resurgence of life in the spring, but not least in the resurrection of Jesus Christ from the dead. We can only understand the significance of these upward movements by faith. We can't *know* that everything has a higher purpose or an eternal destiny, but we can *believe* it because of what God has done through Jesus Christ.

One of my favourite stories is about two caterpillars crawling along the top of a wall on a sunny day. Suddenly a beautiful butterfly fluttered by overhead. Both caterpillars looked up and watched it for a while, then one of them said to the other, 'You'll never catch me going up in one of those things.' Little did it know.

Day 39: Saturday
Lifted up

John 12:20-33

Some Greeks who were in Jerusalem for the Festival told Philip they would like to see Jesus. Philip then took Andrew with him to tell Jesus. But Jesus said, 'The time has come for the Son of Man to be glorified. Unless the grain of wheat falls into the ground and dies, it remains a single seed; but if it dies, it bears much fruit. Whoever loves his life in this world will lose it, but whoever hates his life in this world will keep it to life eternal. Whoever serves me must follow me, so that they may be wherever I am, and the Father will honour them. Now I am deeply troubled, but I can't ask the Father to save me from this hour because it is the very reason why I have come. Father, glorify your name.' Then a voice from heaven said, 'I have glorified it and will glorify it again.' The crowd that heard it said it was thunder, but others said that an angel had spoken to him. Jesus said to them, 'This voice was not for me but for you. The judgement of this world is now here, the prince of this world shall be thrown out, and I, if I be lifted up from the earth, will draw all people to myself.' He said this to show what kind of death he was about to die.

The laws of up and down which we considered yesterday appear again today. But this time Jesus explains that death and burial are part of God's upward plan for the unity of all human life in Christ (or even 'all things' – see Ephesians 1:9, 10). The grain *falls* into the ground and *dies*, but that is the only way in which it can rise to new life and bear much fruit. Without being buried it remains sterile.

So, ironically, Jesus died by being lifted up on a cross, showing that his very death is an essential part of God's upward purpose. Stoning or beheading would not have made that point so well. Not that everyone got the point even then. Paul said that Christ crucified was a scandal to the Jews and foolishness to the Gentiles. A third-century picture of the crucifixion was found on the wall of some officers' quarters in Rome showing a man bowing before a figure with an ass's head hanging on a cross, and the inscription read, 'Alexamenos worships his God'.

Yet, in spite of that, Christ on the cross has continued to fascinate the world for two millennia. He not only lived the way of love, he also died for it, not like suicide bombers who, in dying for what they believe, kill others in the process. But by being raised up on the cross with his arms outstretched Jesus offers his love to all the world, and appeals to us to love one another too.

So the message of the cross is an uplifting one. God did not send his Son to damn the world to hell (the world is quite capable of doing that for itself) but to lift it up to heaven. The crucifixion demonstrates in no uncertain terms that the only thing that can save us from our sins is sacrificial love and Jesus had to die to make it clear that sacrificial love is of the very nature of God.

And that is why Jesus speaks about his death and his glorification in the same breath, because though his death showed the powers of evil at their worst, it also revealed the love of God at its best. Darkness may have covered the earth for three hours on Good Friday, but the light of heaven has burst through from the cross into the world ever since. The powers of darkness are fatally wounded, and it is only a matter of time before the light of Christ crucified draws all humankind to God.

But why is it taking so long? It is 2000 years since Christ died, but the world seems as divided as ever and the forces of evil are still at work. The answers could be that, first, God's timescale is very different from ours, as we can see from the age of his creation and the length of human history so far. Secondly, God may want to include as many generations as possible in his scheme of things and needs the gospel to be spread to people of every culture, and that can only happen when the Church takes its missionary role seriously, not by pointing to itself, with all its flaws and failures, but by pointing to the sacrificial love of Jesus Christ and honouring the light of sacrificial love wherever it may shine in the different cultures of the world.

Day 40: Palm Sunday
The King of Peace

John 12:12-16

The next day a great crowd who had come for the Festival, having heard that Jesus was coming into Jerusalem, took palm branches and went out to meet him. They shouted, 'Hosanna! Blessed be the one who comes in the name of the Lord, the King of Israel.' And Jesus, having found a donkey, sat on it, as it is written, 'Fear not, daughter of Zion. Look! Your King comes sitting on a young donkey.' Now his disciples didn't understand at first, but when Jesus was glorified they remembered that these things were written about him and that they did these things to him.

(See also **Matthew 21:1-11; Mark 11:1-11; Luke 19:28-40**)

All the gospel writers make it clear that when Jesus entered Jerusalem on the first Palm Sunday, he came as a king in fulfilment of prophecy (in particular Zechariah 9:9). But he was a king riding on a donkey, and though the excited crowd may have thought that he was the descendant of David (Matthew 21:9; Mark 11:10) who would re-establish the kingdom of Israel (John 12:13), there was no hint of violence in the crowd, only joy. They threw their clothes on the ground for the donkey to walk over, and cut branches from the trees to wave in the air like banners. It was a spontaneous response to the reputation that had built up around Jesus because of his ministry in Galilee and Judah – 'rejoicing and praising God with a loud voice for all the powerful acts which they had seen' (Luke 19:37).

Jesus had no political programme. He wept over Jerusalem because they didn't know 'the things that make for peace' and this could only end in the destruction of the city (not for the first time). Apart from this, the only peace mentioned by any of the gospel writers in their accounts of Palm Sunday is 'peace in heaven' (Luke 19:38) – but not peace on earth.

So Jesus may have been a king but he was unlike any other king who ever lived. He had no wealth except spiritual wealth, no power except spiritual power, no authority except spiritual authority. For he had come to establish a kingdom which needs none of the trappings of royalty or military weapons or economic power. His throne was a cross and his crown was made of thorns because his kingdom is based on love alone. And that is why it will last for ever.

In 1950, two years before he was forced to abdicate, King Farouk I of Egypt said, 'In a few more years there will only be five kings left in the world: the King of England and the four kings in a pack of cards.' But he'd forgotten King Jesus who rode into Jerusalem on a donkey 2000 years ago and still reigns in his people's hearts and lives today.

> They sometimes say that Jesus was a king,
> and yet he had no throne or golden crown,
> no royal robes or jewelled ring.
> He had no army to enforce his Law;
> his wealth was not in palaces or lands;
> he lived his life among the poor.
>
> Yet, King he is;
> and though he reigns unseen,
> and love's the only power at his command –
> in truth, no greater king has ever been,
> whose love and peace shall rule in every land.[1]

---

1 Revised version of the author's 'King Jesus' in *The Electric Bible* (Kevin Mayhew).

Bible reference index

References are to day numbers, not pages.